PLAYS

BY

AUGUST STRINDBERG

THE DREAM PLAY

THE LINK

THE DANCE OF DEATH, Part I

THE DANCE OF DEATH, Part II

TRANSLATED WITH AN INTRODUCTION BY

EDWIN BJÖRKMAN

NEW YORK

CHARLES SCRIBNER'S SONS

1912

NOTE

This translation is authorised by
Mr. Strindberg, and he has also
approved the selection of the
plays included in this volume.

CONTENTS

INTRODUCTION

To the first volume of his remarkable series of autobiographical novels, August Strindberg gave the name of "The Bondwoman's Son." The allusion was twofold—to his birth and to the position which fate, in his own eyes, seemed to have assigned him both as man and artist.

If we pass on to the third part of his big trilogy, "To Damascus," also an autobiographical work, but written nearly twenty years later, we find *The Stranger*, who is none but the author, saying: "I was the Bondwoman's Son, concerning whom it was writ—'Cast out this bondwoman and her son; for the son of the bondwoman shall not be heir with the free woman's son.'"

And *The Lady*, back of whom we glimpse Strindberg's second wife, replies: "Do you know why Ishmael was cast out? It is to be read a little further back—because he was a scoffer! And then it is also said: 'He will be a wild man; his hand will be against every man, and every man's hand against him; and he shall dwell in opposition to all his brethren.'"

These quotations should be read in conjunction with still another, taken from Strindberg's latest play, "The Great Highway," which, while being a sort of symbolical summary of his life experience, yet pierces the magic circle of self-concern within which too often he has remained a captive. There *The Hermit* asks: "You do not love your fellow-men?" And Strindberg, masquerading as *The Hunter*, cries in answer: "Yes, far too much, and fear them for that reason, too."

3

August Strindberg was born at Stockholm, Sweden, on January 22, 1849. His father was a small tradesman, who had lost his business just before August was born, but who had the energy and ability to start all over again as a steamship agent, making a decided success of his second venture. The success, however, was slow in coming, and the boy's earliest years were spent in the worst kind of poverty—that poverty which has to keep up outward appearances.

The mother had been a barmaid in one of the numerous inns forming one of the Swedish capital's most characteristic features. There the elder Strindberg had met her and fallen deeply in love with her. August was their third child, born a couple of months after their relationship had become legalized in spite of bitter opposition from the husband's family. Other children followed, many of them dying early, so that August could write in later years that one of his first concrete recollections was of the black-jacketed candy which used to be passed around at every Swedish funeral.

Though the parents were always tired, and though the little home was hopelessly overcrowded—ten persons living in three rooms—yet the family life was not without its happiness. Only August seemed to stand apart from the rest, having nothing in common with his parents or with the other children. In fact, a sort of warfare seems to have been raging incessantly between him and his elder brothers. Thus a character naturally timid and reserved had those traits developed to a point where its whole existence seemed in danger of being warped.

At school he was not much happier, and as a rule he regarded the tasks set him there as so much useless drudgery. Always and everywhere he seemed in fear of having his personality violated, until at last that apprehension, years later, took on a form so morbid that it all but carried him across the limits of rationality. With this suspiciousness of his environment went, however, a keen desire to question and to understand. He has said of himself that the predominant traits of his character have been "doubt and sensitiveness to pressure." In these two traits much of his art will, indeed, find its explanation.

At the age of thirteen he lost his mother, and less than a year later his father remarried—choosing for his second wife the former housekeeper. That occurrence made the boy's isolation at home complete. During the years that followed he threw himself with his usual passionate surrender into religious broodings and practices. This mood lasted until he left for the university at Upsala. He was then eighteen. During his first term at the university he was so poor that he could buy no books. Worse even—he could not buy the wood needed to heat the bare garret where he lived.

Returning to Stockholm, he tried to teach in one of the public schools—the very school which he had attended during the unhappiest part of his childhood. From that time dates the theme of eternal repetition, of forced return to past experiences, which recurs constantly in his works. Another recurring theme is that of unjust punishment, and it has also come out of his own life—from an occasion when, as a boy of eight, he was suspected of having drunk some wine that was missing, and when, in spite of his indignant protests, he was held guilty and finally compelled to acknowledge himself so in order to escape further punishment.

But while still teaching school, he made certain acquaintances that set his mind groping for some sort of literary expression. He tried time and again to write verse, only to fail—until one day, in a sort of trance, he found himself shaping words into measured lines, and it suddenly dawned on him that he had accomplished the feat held beyond him.

From the first the stage drew him, and his initial work was a little comedy, concerning which nothing is known now. Then he wrote another one-act play with the Danish sculptor Thorvaldsen for central figure, and this was accepted by the Royal Theatre and actually played with some success. Finally he produced a brief historical play in prose, "The Outlaw," which was spurned by the critics and the public, but which brought him the personal good-will and financial support of King Charles XV.

Thus favoured, he returned to the university with the thought of taking a degree. Instead he read everything not required in the courses, quarrelled with every professor to whom he had to submit himself for examination, and spent the major part of his time with a set of youngsters whose sole ambition was to make literature. Of that coterie, Strindberg was the only one to reach the goal which all dreamt of. On the sudden death of the king, when his little stipend ceased, he went up to the capital again, bent on staying away for ever from the university.

During the next couple of years, he studied medicine for a while, tried himself as an actor, conducted a trade journal, and failed rather than succeeded to make a living as a hack writer for various obscure newspapers. All this life he has pictured with biting humour in his first big novel, "The Red Room." At last, when he was twenty-three and had withdrawn in sheer desperation to one of the little islands between Stockholm and the open sea, he conceived and completed a five-act historical play, named "Master Olof," after Archbishop Olaus Petri, the Luther of Sweden.

The three main figures of that play, *Master Olof, King Gustavus Vasa*, and *Gert the Printer*, were designed by the author to represent three phases of his own character. The *King* was the opportunist, *Olof* the idealist, and *Gert* the "impossibilist." The title first chosen for the play was "The Renegade." It was suggested by the cry with which *Gert* greets the surrender of *Olof* in the final scene.

The indifference shown that first big work came near turning Strindberg away from a literary career for ever. It took him several years to recover from the shock of disappointment—a shock the more severe because he felt so uncertain of his own gifts. But those years of seeming inactivity were not lost. He had obtained a position in the Royal Library, which gave him a living and free access to all the books he wanted. At first he sought forgetfulness in the most exotic studies, such as the Chinese language. The honours of the savant tempted him, and he wrote a monograph which was accepted by the French Institute.

Gradually, however, he was drawn back to his own time. And there was hardly a field of human thought to which he did not give some attention. Already as a student at Upsala, his conception of life had been largely determined by the study of the Danish individualistic philosopher Kierkegaard, the English determinist Buckle, and the German pessimist Eduard von Hartmann. Among novelists, Hugo and Dickens were his favourites. They together with the brothers de Goncourt, and not Zola, helped principally to shape his artistic form until he was strong enough to stand wholly on his own feet.

At the age of twenty-six he met the woman who was to play the double part of muse and fate to him. She was already married. In the end she obtained a divorce and became Strindberg's wife. To begin with they were very happy, and under the stimulus of this unfamiliar feeling Strindberg began once more to write—but now in a manner such that recognition could no longer be denied him. The novel already mentioned was his first popular success. It drew bitter attacks from the conservative elements, but the flavour of real life pervading it conquered all opposition. To this day that first work of social criticism has not been forgiven Strindberg by the official guardians of Swedish literature.

After a while Strindberg threw himself with passion into the study of Swedish history. One of the results was a daring work named "The Swedish People," which is still, next to the Bible, the most read book among the Swedes in this country. He wrote also a series of short stories on historical themes which combined artistic value with a truly remarkable insight into the life of by-gone days. This series was named "Swedish Events and Adventures." About the same time he administered some scathing strictures on social and political conditions in a volume of satirical essays entitled "The New Kingdom."

His plays from this period include "The Secret of the Guild" and "Sir Bengt's Lady," both historical dramas of romantic nature. To these must be added his first fairy play, "The Wanderings of Lucky-Per," concerning which he declared recently that it was meant for children only and must not be counted among his more serious efforts. But this play has from the start been a great favourite with the public, combining in its rapidly moving scenes something of a modern "Everyman" and not a little of a Swedish "Peer Gynt."

After he had resigned from the Royal Library and retired to Switzerland for the purpose of devoting all his time to writing, he produced the volume of short stories, "Marriage," which led him up to the first turning point in his artistic career. It dealt with modern marital conditions in a manner meant to reveal the economic reefs on which so many unions are wrecked. His attitude toward women had already become critical in that work, but it was not yet hostile.

The book was confiscated. Criminal proceedings were brought against its publisher. The charge was that it spoke

offensively of rites held sacred by the established religion of
Sweden. Everybody knew that this was a mere pretext, and
that the true grievance against the book lay in its outspoken
utterances on questions of sex morality. Urged by friends,
Strindberg hastened home and succeeded in assuming the
part of defendant in place of the publisher. The jury freed
him, and the youth of the country proclaimed him their
leader and spokesman.

But the impression left on Strindberg's mind by that epi-
sode was very serious and distinctly unfavourable. As in his
childhood, when he found himself disbelieved though telling
the truth, so he felt now more keenly than anything else the
questioning of his motives, which he knew to be pure. And
the leaders of the feminist movement, then particularly strong
in Sweden, turned against him with a bitterness not surpassed by that which Ibsen had to face from directly opposite
quarters after the publication of "A Doll's House." Add
finally that his marriage, which had begun so auspiciously,
was rapidly changing into torture for both parties concerned
in it.

Yet his growing embitterment did not make itself felt at
once. In 1885 he published four short stories meant to em-
body the onward trend of the modern spirit and the actual
materialisation of some of its fondest dreams. Collectively
he named those stories "Real Utopias," and they went far
toward winning him a reputation in Germany, where he was
then living.

But with the appearance of the second part of "Marriage"
in 1886, it was plain that a change had come over him. Its
eighteen stories constituted an unmistakable protest against
everything for which the feminist movement stood. The
efforts of Ibsen and Björnson to abolish the so-called "double
code of morality"—one for men and another one for women—

were openly challenged on the ground that different results made male and female "immorality" two widely different things. Right here it should be pointed out, however, that Strindberg always, and especially in his later years, has demanded as high a measure of moral purity from men as from women—the real distinction between him and the two great Norwegians lying in the motives on which he based that demand.

The second part of 'Marriage" shows a change not only in spirit but in form, and this change becomes more accentuated in every work published during the next few years. Until then Strindberg had shown strong evidence of the Romantic origin of his art. From now on, and until the ending of the great mental crisis in the later nineties, he must be classed as an ultra-naturalist, with strong materialistic and sceptical leanings. At the same time he becomes more and more individualistic in his social outlook, spurning the mass which, as he then felt, had spurned him. And after a while the works of Nietzsche came to complete what his personal experience had begun. His attitude toward woman, as finally developed during this period, may be summed up in an allegation not only of moral and mental but of biological inferiority. And though during his later life he has retracted much and softened more of what he said in those years of rampant masculine rebellion, he continues to this day to regard women as an intermediary biological form, standing between the man and the child.

With the publication, in 1887, of "The Father," a modern three-act tragedy, Strindberg reached a double climax. That work has been hailed as one of his greatest, if not the greatest, as far as technical perfection is concerned. At the same time it presents that duel of the sexes—which to him had taken the place of love—in its most startling and hideous aspects.

The gloom of the play is almost unsurpassed. The ingeniousness of its plot may well be called infernal. By throwing doubt on her husband's rights as father of the child held to be theirs in common, the woman in the play manages to undermine the reason of a strong and well-balanced man until he becomes transformed into a raving maniac.

"The Comrades," a modern four-act comedy, portrays the marriage of two artists and shows the woman as a mental parasite, drawing both her inspiration and her skill from the husband, whom she tries to shake off when she thinks him no longer needed for her success. Then came the play of his which is perhaps the most widely known—I mean the realistic drama which, for want of a better English equivalent, must be named here "Miss Juliet." It embodied some startling experiments in form and has undoubtedly exercised a distinct influence on the subsequent development of dramatic technique. On the surface it appears to offer little more than another version of the sex duel, but back of the conflict between man and woman we discover another one, less deep-going perhaps, but rendered more acute by existing conditions. It is the conflict between the upper and partly outlived elements of society and its still unrefined, but vitally unimpaired, strata. And it is the stronger vitality, here represented by the man, which carries the day.

The rest of Strindberg's dramatic productions during this middle, naturalistic period, lasting from 1885 to 1894, included eight more one-act plays, several of which rank very high, and another fairy play, "The Keys to Heaven," which probably marks his nearest approach to a purely negative conception of life.

Paralleling the plays, we find a series of novels and short stories dealing with the people on those islands where Strindberg fifteen years earlier had written his "Master Olof."

Two things make these works remarkable: first, the rare understanding shown in them of the life led by the tough race that exists, so to speak, between land and sea; and secondly, their genuine humour, which at times, as in the little story named "The Tailor Has a Dance," rises into almost epic expression. The last of these novels, "At the Edge of the Sea," embodies Strindberg's farthest advance into Nietzschean dreams of supermanhood. But led by his incorruptible logic, he is forced to reduce those dreams to the absurdity which they are sure to involve whenever the superman feels himself standing apart from ordinary humanity.

Finally he wrote, during the earlier part of this marvellously prolific period, five autobiographical novels. One of these was not published until years later. Three others were collectively known as "The Bondwoman's Son," and carried his revelations up to the time of his marriage. The first volume in the series is especially noteworthy because of its searching and sympathetic study of child psychology. But all the novels in this series are of high value because of the sharp light they throw on social conditions. Strindberg's power as an acute and accurate observer has never been questioned, and it has rarely been more strikingly evidenced than in his autobiographical writings. A place by itself, though belonging to the same series, is held by "A Fool's Confession," wherein Strindberg laid bare the tragedy of his first marriage. It is the book that has exposed him to more serious criticism than any other. He wrote it in French and consented to its publication only as a last means of escaping unendurable financial straits. Against his vain protests, unauthorised translations were brought out in German and Swedish.

The dissolution of his marriage occurred in 1891. The circumstances surrounding that break were extremely painful to Strindberg. Both the facts of the legal procedure and the

feelings it evoked within himself have been almost photo-
graphically portrayed in the one-act play, "The Link," which
forms part of this volume.   The "link" which binds man and
woman together even when their love is gone and the law has
severed all external ties is the child—and it is always for the
offspring that Strindberg reserves his tenderest feelings and
greatest concern.

After the divorce Strindberg left for Germany, where his
works in the meantime had been making steady headway.
A couple of years later he was taken up in France, and there
was a time during the first half of the nineties, when he had
plays running simultaneously at half a dozen Parisian theatres.
While at Berlin, he met a young woman writer of Austrian
birth who soon after became his second wife.   Their marriage lasted only a few years, and while it was not as unhappy as the first one, it helped to bring on the mental crisis
for which Strindberg had been heading ever since the prosecution of "Marriage," in 1884.

He ceased entirely to write and plunged instead into scientific speculation and experimentation.   Chemistry was the
subject that had the greatest fascination for him, and his
dream was to prove the transmutability of the elements.   In
the course of a prolonged stay at Paris, where he shunned
everybody and risked both health and life in his improvised
laboratory, his mental state became more and more abnormal, without ever reaching a point where he ceased to realise just what was going on within himself.   He began to
have psychic experiences of a character that to him appeared
distinctly supernatural.   At the same time he was led by
the reading of Balzac to the discovery of Swedenborg.   By
quick degrees, though not without much mental suffering, he
rejected all that until then had to him represented life's
highest truths.   From being a materialistic sceptic, he be-

came a believing mystic, to whom this world seemed a mere
transitory state of punishment, a "hell" created by his own
thoughts.

The crisis took him in the end to a private sanitarium kept
by an old friend in the southern part of Sweden, but it would
be far from safe to assume that he ever reached a state of
actual insanity. His return to health began in 1896 and was
completed in a year. In 1897 he resumed his work of artistic
creation once more, and with a new spirit that startled those
who had held him lost for ever. First of all a flood of personal
experiences and impressions needed expression. This he accomplished by his two autobiographical novels, "Inferno"
and "Legends," the former of which must be counted one
of the most remarkable studies in abnormal psychology in
the world's literature. Next came "The Link" and another
one-act play. In 1898 he produced the first two parts of
"To Damascus," a play that—in strikingly original form, and
with a depth of thought and feeling not before achieved—
embodied his own soul's long pilgrimage in search of internal
and external harmony. The last part of the trilogy was not
added until 1904.

Then followed ten years of production so amazing that it
surpassed his previous high-water mark during the middle
eighties, both in quality and quantity. Once for all the
mood and mode of his creation had been settled. He was
still a realist in so far as faithfulness to life was concerned,
but the reality for which he had now begun to strive was
spiritual rather than material. He can, during this final
period, only be classed as a symbolist, but of the kind typi-
fied by Ibsen in the series of masterpieces beginning with
"Rosmersholm" and ending with "Little Eyolf."

More and more as he pushes on from one height to another,
he manages to fuse the two offices of artist and moralist with-

out injury to either of them. His view of life is still pessi-
mistic, but back of man's earthly disappointments and humiliations and sufferings he glimpses a higher existence to which
this one serves merely as a preparation. Everything that
happens to himself and to others seems to reveal the per-
sistent influence of secret powers, pulling and pushing, re-
warding and punishing, but always urging and leading man
to some goal not yet bared to his conscious vision. Resignation, humility, kindness become the main virtues of human
existence. And the greatest tragedy of that existence he sees
in man's—that is, his own—failure to make all his actions con-
form to those ideals. Thus, in the closing line of his last
play, "The Great Highway," he pleads for mercy as one who
has suffered more than most "from the inability to be that
which we will to be."

Among the earliest results of his autumnal renascence was
a five-act historical drama named "Gustavus Vasa." It
proved the first of a dozen big plays dealing with the main
events in his country's history from the fifteenth to the eighteenth century. As a rule they were built about a monarch
whose reign marked some national crisis. Five stand out
above the rest in artistic value: "Gustavus Vasa," "Eric
XIV," "Gustavus Adolphus," "Charles XII," and "The
Last Knight." At once intensely national and broadly human in their spirit, these plays won for Strindberg a higher
place in his countrymen's hearts than he had ever before
held—though notes of discord were not missing on account of
the freedom with which he exposed and demolished false
idols and outlived national ideals. As they stand to-day,
those dramas have in them so much of universal appeal that
I feel sure they must sooner or later win the same attention
in the English-speaking countries that they have already
received in Germany.

While thus recalling the past to new life, he was also busy with another group of plays embodying what practically amounts to a new dramatic form. The literary tendency underlying them might be defined as realistic symbolism or impressionistic mysticism—you can take your choice! The characters in those plays are men and women very much belonging to our own day. They speak as you or I might do. And yet there is in them and about them a significance surpassing not only that of the ordinary individual, but also that of ordinary poetical portrayals of such individuals.

"There Are Crimes and Crimes," "Christmas," "Easter," and "Midsummer" are the principal plays belonging to this group. With them must be classed the trio of fairy or "dream" plays written under the acknowledged influence of Maeterlinck. In the first of these, the charming dramatic legend named "Swanwhite," the impetus received from the Belgian makes itself clearly felt. In the last of them, "The Dream Play," Strindberg has worked out a form that is wholly new and wholly his own. As the play in question forms part of this volume, I shall not need to speak of it here in the manner it would otherwise deserve.

Related to the group just described, and yet not confinable within it, stands the double drama, "The Dance of Death," which also appears in this volume. Numerous critics have declared it Strindberg's greatest play, and there is much in the work to warrant such a judgment. Its construction is masterly. Its characters are almost shockingly real. And yet the play as a whole is saturated with that sense of larger relationships which we are wont to dispose of by calling it "mysticism." Like all of Strindberg's work belonging to this period, it constitutes a huge piece of symbolism—but the subject of its symbolical interpretation seems to be nothing less than the sum of human interrelationships.

During the last three or four years of the decade we are now dealing with, Strindberg was very much interested in the project of establishing a theatre at Stockholm, where nothing but his own productions were to be staged. The plan was actually carried out and a building arranged that held only about two hundred people. It was called the Intimate Theatre. There Strindberg made some highly interesting experiments in the simplification and standardising of scenery, until at last some of his plays were given with no other accessories than draperies. The effects thus obtained proved unexpectedly successful. For this stage Strindberg wrote five dramas which he defined as "chamber plays." In form they harked back to "Miss Juliet," and they were meant to be played without interruptions. But in spirit they were marked by the same blend of mysticism and realism that forms such a striking feature of "The Dream Play," for instance. Add to these another fairy play, "The Slippers of Abu Casem," and a final autobiographical drama named "The Great Highway," and we get a total of twenty-nine dramatic works in ten years.[1]

But at the same time Strindberg's pen was no less active in other fields. There are two more autobiographical volumes, two novels displaying vast social canvasses, four collections of short stories, and one collection of poems; also three bulky volumes named collectively "The Blue Books" and containing the most wonderful medley of scientific speculations, philosophical pronouncements, personal polemics, and aphoristic embodiments of the author's rich store of wisdom; and finally a score of pamphlets—analytical studies of Shakespeare plays, instructions to the members of the Intimate Theatre, satirical

[1] For more critical treatment of Strindberg's art I would refer the reader to my articles in *The Forum* of February and March, 1912.

studies of contemporary social and literary conditions, propositions for a more complete democratisation of the government, and so on almost endlessly. And notwithstanding much supercilious criticism as well as some warranted regrets for the tone at times employed in these works, it is pretty generally admitted that Strindberg never has approached any topic without saying something worth while about it.

Outwardly Strindberg's life has been very quiet since he returned to his native country in 1897. A third marriage, contracted in 1901 and dissolved three years later, served only to reconcile him once for all to the solitude that has always surrounded him more or less, even in the midst of admiring or condemning multitudes. He is now sixty-three years old, and the last news indicates that, at last, his iron health is failing him. In the sheltered nook which he has established for himself at Stockholm, he busies himself with philological studies, interrupted mainly by visits from his children, of which there are five from the three marriages. Two of these—his eldest daughter, who is now happily married, and the youngest, a vivacious lass of nine to whom "The Slippers of Abu Casem" was dedicated—are in the habit of calling daily. Flowers and music are what he loves next to his children and his work. From that corner where he hears nothing but echoes of the storms that are still raging at times about his public utterances, he follows with keen eye whatever is happening in the world of deeds as well as in the world of letters. And in the meantime his fame is steadily spreading and growing. On the European continent his name is constantly mentioned together with those of Ibsen and Björnson. In the English-speaking countries it has hitherto remained merely a name. The time has surely come for a realisation of some of the things that name stands for, and it is my earnest hope that this volume may help to change a condition that reflects more on those who do not know than on him who is not known.

In regard to the style of my translations, I wish to quote some words written before the task now finished had ever been suggested to me. They are from an article on "Slaughtering Strindberg," which appeared in "The Drama," of August, 1911:

"Strindberg is the man who has raised modern Swedish to its utmost potency of beauty and power. It may also be said, and with equal truth, that he has made the literary language of this country truly modern. This he has achieved not by polishing study-born mannerisms, but by watching and developing the living idiom that flows from the lips of men and women around him—observed at home and in the office, on the street and in the restaurant, while loving and dying, while chatting and quarrelling. Never was a man more keen on catching the life breath of his own time, and never was a man more scornful of mere fads and fashions, born one moment and forgotten in the next. To transplant the work of such a man may be difficult, but it involves no impossibility, provided only that we observe his own practical attitude toward what constitutes 'good form' and 'bad form' in a pulsing and growing language. We, on this side of the ocean, ought to be able to read Strindberg and receive impressions virtually identical with those received by a Swedish reader at Stockholm. And I believe that it will be easier to find equivalents for his clean-cut and flexible prose out of what is called English here than out of what bears that name in England."

Finally, I wish to mention that the prologue now attached to "The Dream Play" has never before been published in any language. It was written last year as an afterthought, and was by the author kindly placed at my disposal in manuscript.

A CHRONOLOGICAL LIST OF AUGUST STRINDBERG'S MAIN WORKS

Plays: "Hermione," 1869; "The Outlaw," 1871; "Master Olof," 1872; "The Secret of the Guild," 1880; "Sir Bengt's Lady," 1882; "The Wanderings of Lucky-Per," 1883; "The Father," 1887; "The Comrades," 1888; "Miss Juliet," 1888; "Creditors," 1890; "Pariah," 1890; "Samum," 1890; "The Stronger," 1890; "The Keys of Heaven," 1892; "The First Warning," 1893; "Debit and Credit," 1893; "Mother-Love," 1893; "Facing Death," 1893; "Playing with Fire," 1897; "The Link," 1897; "To Damascus," I and II, 1898; "There are Crimes and Crimes," 1899; "Christmas," 1899; "Gustavus Vasa," 1899; "Eric XIV," 1899; "The Saga of the Folkungs," 1899; "Gustavus Adolphus," 1900; "The Dance of Death," I and II, 1901; "Easter," 1901; "Midsummer," 1901; "Engelbreckt," 1901; "Charles XII," 1901; "The Crown Bride," 1902; "Swanwhite," 1902; "The Dream Play," 1902; "Gustavus III," 1903; "Queen Christina," 1903; "The Nightingale of Wittenberg," 1903; "To Damascus," III, 1904; "Storm," 1907; "The Burned Lot," 1907; "The Spook Sonata," 1907; "The Pelican," 1907; "The Slippers of Abu Casem," 1908; "The Last Knight," 1908; "The National Director," 1909; "The Earl of Bjällbo," 1909; "The Black Glove," 1909; "The Great Highway," 1909.

Novels and Short-story Collections: "The Red Room," 1879; "Swedish Events and Adventures," 1882–91; "Marriage," I, 1884; "Real Utopias," 1885; "Marriage," II, 1886; "The People at Hemsö," 1887, "Fisher Folks," 1888; "Chandalah," 1889; "At the Edge of the Sea," 1890; "Fables," 1890–7; "Sagas," 1903; "The Gothic Rooms," 1904; "Historical Miniatures," 1905; "New Swedish Events," 1906; "Black Flags," 1907; "The Scapegoat," 1907.

Autobiographical Fiction: "The Bondwoman's Son," I–III, 1886–7, "The Author," 1887; "A Fool's Confession," 1888; "Inferno," 1897, "Legends," 1898; "Fairhaven and Foulstrand," 1902; "Alone," 1903.

History, Essays, Etc.: "The New Kingdom," 1882; "The Swedish People," 1882; "Little Studies of Plants and Animals," 1888; "Among French Peasants," 1889; "A Blue Book," I–III, 1907–8; "Speeches to the Swedish Nation," 1910; "Religious Renascence," 1910; "The Origins of Our Mother Tongue," 1910; "Biblical Proper Names," 1910.

A REMINDER

As he did in his previous dream play,[1] so in this one the author has tried to imitate the disconnected but seemingly logical form of the dream. Anything may happen; everything is possible and probable. Time and space do not exist. On an insignificant background of reality, imagination designs and embroiders novel patterns: a medley of memories, experiences, free fancies, absurdities and improvisations.

The characters split, double, multiply, vanish, solidify, blur, clarify. But one consciousness reigns above them all— that of the dreamer; and before it there are no secrets, no incongruities, no scruples, no laws. There is neither judgment nor exoneration, but merely narration. And as the dream is mostly painful, rarely pleasant, a note of melancholy and of pity with all living things runs right through the wabbly tale. Sleep, the liberator, plays often a dismal part, but when the pain is at its worst, the awakening comes and reconciles the sufferer with reality, which, however distressing it may be, nevertheless seems happy in comparison with the torments of the dream.

[1] The trilogy "To Damascus."

PROLOGUE

*The background represents cloud banks that resemble corroding
slate cliffs with ruins of castles and fortresses.*

*The constellations of Leo, Virgo, and Libra are visible, and
from their midst the planet Jupiter is shining with a strong
light.*

THE DAUGHTER OF INDRA *stands on the topmost
cloud.*

THE VOICE OF INDRA [*from above*].

Where are you, daughter, where?

THE DAUGHTER.

Here, father, here.

THE VOICE.

You've lost your way, my child—beware, you sink—
How got you there?

THE DAUGHTER.

I followed from ethereal heights the ray
Of lightning, and for car a cloud I took—
It sank, and now my journey downward tends.
O, noble father, Indra, tell what realms
I now draw near? The air is here so close,
And breathing difficult.

THE VOICE.

Behind you lies the second world; the third
Is where you stand. From Çukra, morning star

25

You have withdrawn yourself to enter soon
The vapoury circle of the earth. For mark
The Seventh House you take. It's Libra called:
There stands the day-star in the balanced hour
When Fall gives equal weight to night and day.

THE DAUGHTER.

You named the earth—is that the ponderous world
And dark, that from the moon must take its light?

THE VOICE.

It is the heaviest and densest sphere
Of all that travel through the space.

THE DAUGHTER.

And is it never brightened by the sun?

THE VOICE.

Of course, the sun does reach it—now and then——

THE DAUGHTER.

There is a rift, and downward goes my glance——

THE VOICE.

What sees my child?

THE DAUGHTER.

I see—O beautiful!—with forests green,
With waters blue, white peaks, and yellow fields——

THE VOICE.

Yes, beautiful as all that Brahma made—
But still more beautiful it was of yore,
In primal morn of ages. Then occurred
Some strange mishap; the orbit was disturbed;
Rebellion led to crime that called for check——

THE DAUGHTER.

Now from below I hear some sounds arise—
What sort of race is dwelling there?

THE VOICE.

> See for yourself—Of Brahma's work no ill
> I say: but what you hear, it is their speech.

THE DAUGHTER.

> It sounds as if—it has no happy ring!

THE VOICE.

> I fear me not—for even their mother-tongue
> Is named complaint. A race most hard to please,
> And thankless, are the dwellers on the earth——

THE DAUGHTER.

> O, say not so—for I hear cries of joy,
> Hear noise and thunder, see the lightnings flash—
> Now bells are ringing, fires are lit,
> And thousand upon thousand tongues
> Sing praise and thanks unto the heavens on high—
> Too harshly, father, you are judging them.

THE VOICE.

> Descend, that you may see and hear, and then
> Return and let me know if their complaints
> And wailings have some reasonable ground——

THE DAUGHTER.

> Well then, I go; but, father, come with me.

THE VOICE.

> No, there below I cannot breathe——

THE DAUGHTER.

> Now sinks the cloud—what sultriness—I choke!
> I am not breathing air, but smoke and steam—
> With heavy weight it drags me down,
> And I can feel already how it rolls—
> Indeed, the best of worlds is not the third——

THE VOICE.
>The best I cannot call it, nor the worst.
>Its name is Dust; and like them all, it rolls:
>And therefore dizzy sometimes grows the race,
>And seems to be half foolish and half mad—
>Take courage, child—a trial, that is all!

THE DAUGHTER. [*Kneeling as the cloud sinks downward*]
>I sink!

Curtain.

THE DREAM PLAY

*The background represents a forest of gigantic hollyhocks in
bloom. They are white, pink, crimson, sulphureous, vio-
let; and above their tops is seen the gilded roof of a castle,
the apex of which is formed by a bud resembling a crown.
At the foot of the castle walls stand a number of straw ricks,
and around these stable litter is scattered. The side-scenes,
which remain unchanged throughout the play, show con-
ventionalised frescoes, suggesting at once internal decora-
tion, architecture, and landscape.*

Enter THE GLAZIER *and* THE DAUGHTER.

THE DAUGHTER. The castle is growing higher and higher
above the ground. Do you see how much it has grown since
last year?

THE GLAZIER. [*To himself*] I have never seen this castle
before—have never heard of a castle that grew, but—[*To* THE
DAUGHTER, *with firm conviction*] Yes, it has grown two yards,
but that is because they have manured it—and if you notice, it
has put out a wing on the sunny side.

THE DAUGHTER. Ought it not to be blooming soon, as we
are already past midsummer?

THE GLAZIER. Don't you see the flower up there?

THE DAUGHTER. Yes, I see! [*Claps her hands*] Say, father, why do flowers grow out of dirt?

THE GLAZIER. [*Simply*] Because they do not feel at home
in the dirt, and so they make haste to get up into the light
in order to blossom and die.

29

THE DAUGHTER. Do you know who lives in that castle?

THE GLAZIER. I have known it, but cannot remember.

THE DAUGHTER. I believe a prisoner is kept there—and he must be waiting for me to set him free.

THE GLAZIER. And what is he to pay for it?

THE DAUGHTER. One does not bargain about one's duty. Let us go into the castle.

THE GLAZIER. Yes, let us go in.

They go toward the background, which opens and slowly disappears to either side.

The stage shows now a humble, bare room, containing only a table and a few chairs. On one of the chairs sits an officer, dressed in a very unusual yet modern uniform. He is tilting the chair backward and beating the table with his sabre.

THE DAUGHTER. [*Goes to the officer, from whose hand she gently takes the sabre*] Don't! Don't!

THE OFFICER. Oh, Agnes dear, let me keep the sabre.

THE DAUGHTER. No, you break the table. [*To* THE GLAZIER] Now you go down to the harness-room and fix that window pane. We'll meet later.

[THE GLAZIER *goes out.*

THE DAUGHTER. You are imprisoned in your own rooms— I have come to set you free.

THE OFFICER. I have been waiting for you, but I was not sure you were willing to do it.

THE DAUGHTER. The castle is strongly built; it has seven walls, but—it can be done!—Do you want it, or do you not?

THE OFFICER. Frankly speaking, I cannot tell—for in either case I shall suffer pain. Every joy that life brings has to be paid for with twice its measure of sorrow. It is hard to stay where I am, but if I buy the sweets of freedom, then I shall have to suffer twice as much—Agnes, I'll rather endure it as it is, if I can only see you.

THE DAUGHTER. What do you see in me?

THE OFFICER. Beauty, which is the harmony of the universe—There are lines of your body which are nowhere to be found, except in the orbits of the solar system, in strings that are singing softly, or in the vibrations of light—You are a child of heaven——

THE DAUGHTER. So are you.

THE OFFICER. Why must I then keep horses, tend stable, and cart straw?

THE DAUGHTER. So that you may long to get away from here.

THE OFFICER. I am longing, but it is so hard to find one's way out.

THE DAUGHTER. But it is a duty to seek freedom in the light.

THE OFFICER. Duty? Life has never recognised any duties toward me.

THE DAUGHTER. You feel yourself wronged by life?

THE OFFICER. Yes, it has been unjust——

Now voices are heard from behind a partition, which a moment later is pulled away. THE OFFICER and THE DAUGHTER look in that direction and stop as if paralysed in the midst of a gesture.

At a table sits THE MOTHER, *looking very sick. In front of her a tallow candle is burning, and every little while she trims it with a pair of snuffers. The table is piled with new-made shirts, and these she is marking with a quill and ink. To the left stands a brown-coloured wardrobe.*

THE FATHER. [*Holds out a silk mantilla toward* THE MOTHER *and says gently*] You don't want it?

THE MOTHER. A silk mantilla for me, my dear—of what use would that be when I am going to die shortly?

THE FATHER. Do you believe what the doctor says?

THE MOTHER. Yes, I believe also what he says, but still more what the voice says in here.

THE FATHER. [*Sadly*] It is true then?—And you are thinking of your children first and last.

THE MOTHER. That has been my life and my reason for living—my joy and my sorrow——

THE FATHER. Christine, forgive me—everything!

THE MOTHER. What have I to forgive? Dearest, you forgive *me!* We have been tormenting each other. Why? That we may not know. We couldn't do anything else—However, here is the new linen for the children. See that they change twice a week—Wednesdays and Sundays—and that Louise washes them—their whole bodies—Are you going out?

THE FATHER. I have to be in the Department at eleven o'clock.

THE MOTHER. Ask Alfred to come in before you go.

THE FATHER. [*Pointing to* THE OFFICER] Why, he is standing right there, dear heart.

THE MOTHER. So my eyes are failing, too—Yes, it is turning dark. [*Trims the candle*] Come here, Alfred.

> THE FATHER *goes out through the middle of the wall, nodding good-bye as he leaves.*
> THE OFFICER *goes over to* THE MOTHER.

THE MOTHER. Who is that girl?

THE OFFICER. [*Whispers*] It is Agnes.

THE MOTHER. Oh, is that Agnes?—Do you know what they say?—That she is a daughter of the god Indra who has asked leave to descend to the earth in order that she may find out what the conditions of men are—But don't say anything about it.

THE OFFICER. A child of the gods, indeed!

THE MOTHER. [*Aloud*] My Alfred, I must soon part from

you and from the other children—But let me first speak a word to you that bears on all the rest of your life.

THE OFFICER. [*Sadly*] Speak, mother.

THE MOTHER. Only a word: don't quarrel with God!

THE OFFICER. What do you mean, mother?

THE MOTHER. Don't go around feeling that life has wronged you.

THE OFFICER. But when I am treated unjustly——

THE MOTHER. You are thinking of the time when you were unjustly punished for having taken a penny that later turned up?

THE OFFICER. Yes, and that one wrong gave a false twist to my whole life——

THE MOTHER. Perhaps. But please take a look into that wardrobe now——

THE OFFICER. [*Embarrassed*] You know, then? It is——

THE MOTHER. The Swiss Family Robinson—for which——

THE OFFICER. Don't say any more!

THE MOTHER. For which your brother was punished—and which you had torn and hidden away.

THE OFFICER. Just think that the old wardrobe is still standing there after twenty years— We have moved so many times, and my mother died ten years ago.

THE MOTHER. Yes, and what of it? You are always asking all sorts of questions, and in that way you spoil the better part of your life—There is Lena, now.

LENA. [*Enters*] Thank you very much, ma'am, but I can't go to the baptism.

THE MOTHER. And why not, my girl?

LENA. I have nothing to put on.

THE MOTHER. I'll let you use my mantilla here

LENA. Oh, no, ma'am, that wouldn't do!

THE MOTHER. Why not?— It is not likely that I'll go to any more parties.

THE OFFICER. And what will father say? It is a present from him——

THE MOTHER. What small minds——

THE FATHER. [*Puts his head through the wall*] Are you going to lend my present to the servant girl?

THE MOTHER. Don't talk that way! Can you not remember that I was a servant girl also? Why should you offend one who has done nothing?

THE FATHER. Why should you offend me, your husband?

THE MOTHER. Oh, this life! If you do anything nice, there is always somebody who finds it nasty. If you act kindly to one, it hurts another. Oh, this life!

> *She trims the candle so that it goes out. The stage turns dark and the partition is pushed back to its former position.*

THE DAUGHTER. Men are to be pitied.

THE OFFICER. You think so?

THE DAUGHTER. Yes, life is hard—but love overcomes everything. You shall see for yourself.

> [*They go toward the background.*
> *The background is raised and a new one revealed, showing an old, dilapidated party-wall. In the centre of it is a gate closing a passageway. This opens upon a green, sunlit space, where is seen a tremendous blue monk's-hood (aconite). To the left of the gate sits* THE PORTRESS. *Her head and shoulders are covered by a shawl, and she is crocheting at a bed-spread with a star-like pattern. To the right of the gate is a billboard, which* THE BILLPOSTER *is cleaning. Beside him stands a dipnet with a green pole. Further to the right is a door that has an air-hole shaped like a*

four-leaved clover. To the left of the gate stands a small linden tree with coal-black trunk and a few pale-green leaves. Near it is a small air-hole leading into a cellar.[1]

THE DAUGHTER. [*Going to* THE PORTRESS] Is the spread not done yet?

THE PORTRESS. No, dear. Twenty-six years on such a piece of work is not much.

THE DAUGHTER. And your lover never came back?

THE PORTRESS. No, but it was not his fault. He had to go—poor thing! That was thirty years ago now.

THE DAUGHTER. [*To* THE BILLPOSTER] She belonged to the ballet? Up there in the opera-house?

THE BILLPOSTER. She was number one—but when *he* went, it was as if her dancing had gone with him—and so she didn't get any more parts.

THE DAUGHTER. Everybody complains—with their eyes, at least, and often with words also——

THE BILLPOSTER. I don't complain very much—not now, since I have a dipnet and a green cauf[2]——

THE DAUGHTER. And that can make you happy?

THE BILLPOSTER. Oh, I'm so happy, so— It was the dream of my youth, and now it has come true. Of course, I have grown to be fifty years——

THE DAUGHTER. Fifty years for a dipnet and a cauf——

THE BILLPOSTER. A *green* cauf—mind you, *green*——

THE DAUGHTER. [*To* THE PORTRESS] Let me have the shawl now, and I shall sit here and watch the human children. But you must stand behind me and tell me about everything.

[*She takes the shawl and sits down at the gate.*

[1] Though the author says nothing about it here, subsequent stage directions indicate a door and a window behind the place occupied by THE PORTRESS. Both lead into her room or lodge, which contains a telephone.

[2] A floating wooden box with holes in it used to hold fish.

THE PORTRESS. This is the last day, and the house will be closed up for the season. This is the day when they learn whether their contracts are to be renewed.

THE DAUGHTER. And those that fail of engagement——

THE PORTRESS. O, Lord have mercy! I pull the shawl over my head not to see them.

THE DAUGHTER. Poor human creatures!

THE PORTRESS. Look, here comes one—She's not one of the chosen. See, how she cries.

> THE SINGER *enters from the right; rushes through the gate with her handkerchief to her eyes; stops for a moment in the passageway beyond the gate and leans her head against the wall; then out quickly.*

THE DAUGHTER. Men are to be pitied!

THE PORTRESS. But look at this one. That's the way a happy person looks.

> THE OFFICER *enters through the passageway; dressed in Prince Albert coat and high hat, and carrying a bunch of roses in one hand; he is radiantly happy.*

THE PORTRESS. He's going to marry Miss Victoria.

THE OFFICER. [*Far down on the stage, looks up and sings*] Victoria!

THE PORTRESS. The young lady will be coming in a moment.

THE OFFICER. Good! The carriage is waiting, the table is set, the wine is on ice— Oh, permit me to embrace you, ladies! [*He embraces* THE PORTRESS *and* THE DAUGHTER. *Sings*] Victoria!

A WOMAN'S VOICE FROM ABOVE. [*Sings*] I am here!

THE DAUGHTER. Do you know me?

THE OFFICER. No, I know one woman only—Victoria. Seven years I have come here to wait for her—at noon, when the sun touched the chimneys, and at night, when it was growing dark. Look at the asphalt here, and you will see the path worn by the steps of a faithful lover. Hooray! She is mine. [*Sings*] Victoria! [*There is no reply*] Well, she is dressing, I suppose. [*To* THE BILLPOSTER] There is the dipnet, I see. Everybody belonging to the opera is crazy about dipnets—or rather about fishes—because the fishes are dumb and cannot sing!— What is the price of a thing like that?

THE BILLPOSTER. It is rather expensive.

THE OFFICER. [*Sings*] Victoria! [*Shakes the linden tree*] Look, it is turning green once more. For the eighth time. [*Sings*] Victoria!— Now she is fixing her hair. [*To* THE DAUGHTER] Look here, madam, could I not go up and get my bride?

THE PORTRESS. Nobody is allowed on the stage.

THE OFFICER. Seven years I have been coming here. Seven times three hundred and sixty-five makes two thousand five hundred and fifty-five. [*Stops and pokes at the door with the four-leaved clover hole*] And I have been looking two thousand five hundred and fifty-five times at that door without discovering where it leads. And that clover leaf which is to let in light—for whom is the light meant? Is there anybody within? Does anybody live there?

THE PORTRESS. I don't know. I have never seen it opened.

THE OFFICER. It looks like a pantry door which I saw once when I was only four years old and went visiting with the maid on a Sunday afternoon. We called at several houses—on other maids—but I did not get beyond the kitchen anywhere, and I had to sit between the water barrel and the salt box. I have seen so many kitchens in my days, and the pantry was always just outside, with small round holes bored in the door, and one big hole like a clover leaf— But there cannot be any pantry in the opera-house as they have no kitchen. [*Sings*] Victoria!— Tell me, madam, could she have gone out any other way?

THE PORTRESS. No, there is no other way.

THE OFFICER. Well, then I shall see her here.

> STAGE PEOPLE *rush out and are closely watched by* THE
> OFFICER *as they pass.*

THE OFFICER. Now she must soon be coming— Madam, that blue monk's-hood outside—I have seen it since I was a child. Is it the same ?— I remember it from a country rectory where I stopped when I was seven years old— There are two doves, two blue doves, under the hood—but that time a bee came flying and went into the hood. Then I thought: now I have you! And I grabbed hold of the flower. But the sting of the bee went through it, and I cried—but then the rector's wife came and put damp dirt on the sting—and we had strawberries and cream for dinner— I think it is getting dark already. [*To* THE BILLPOSTER] Where are you going?

THE BILLPOSTER. Home for supper.

THE OFFICER. [*Draws his hand across his eyes*] Evening? At this time ?— O, please, may I go in and telephone to the Growing Castle?

THE DAUGHTER. What do you want there?

THE OFFICER. I am going to tell the Glazier to put in double windows, for it will soon be winter, and I am feeling horribly cold.   [*Goes into the gatekeeper's lodge.*

THE DAUGHTER. Who is Miss Victoria?

THE PORTRESS. His sweetheart.

THE DAUGHTER. Right said! What she is to us and others matters nothing to him. And what she is to him, that alone is her real self.

> *It is suddenly turning dark.*

THE PORTRESS. [*Lights a lantern*] It is growing dark early to-day.

THE DAUGHTER. To the gods a year is as a minute.

THE PORTRESS. And to men a minute may be as long as a year.

THE OFFICER. [*Enters again, looking dusty; the roses are withered*] She has not come yet?

THE PORTRESS. No.

THE OFFICER. But she will come— She will come! [*Walks up and down*] But come to think of it, perhaps I had better call off the dinner after all—as it is late? Yes, I will do that.

[*Goes back into the lodge and telephones.*

THE PORTRESS. [*To* THE DAUGHTER] Can I have my shawl back now?

THE DAUGHTER. No, dear, be free a while. I shall attend to your duties—for I want to study men and life, and see whether things really are as bad as they say.

THE PORTRESS. But it won't do to fall asleep here—never sleep night or day——

THE DAUGHTER. No sleep at night?

THE PORTRESS. Yes, if you are able to get it, but only with the bell string tied around the wrist—for there are night watchmen on the stage, and they have to be relieved every third hour.

THE DAUGHTER. But that is torture!

THE PORTRESS. So you think, but people like us are glad enough to get such a job, and if you only knew how envied I am——

THE DAUGHTER. Envied?— Envy for the tortured?

THE PORTRESS. Yes— But I can tell you what is harder than all drudging and keeping awake nights, harder to bear than draught and cold and dampness—it is to receive the confidences of all the unhappy people up there— They all come to me. Why? Perhaps they read in the wrinkles of my face some runes that are graved by suffering and that invite confessions— In that shawl, dear, lie hidden thirty years of my own and other people's agonies.

THE DAUGHTER. It is heavy, and it burns like nettles.

THE PORTRESS. As it is your wish, you may wear it. When it grows too burdensome, call me, and I shall relieve you.

THE DAUGHTER. Good-bye. What can be done by you ought not to surpass my strength.

THE PORTRESS. We shall see!— But be kind to my poor friends, and don't grow impatient of their complaints.

[*She disappears through the passageway. Complete darkness covers the stage, and while it lasts the scene is changed so that the linden tree appears stripped of all its leaves. Soon the blue monk's-hood is withered, and when the light returns, the verdure in the open space beyond the passageway has changed into autumnal brown.*

THE OFFICER. [*Enters when it is light again. He has gray hair and a gray beard. His clothes are shabby, his collar is soiled and wrinkled. Nothing but the bare stems remain of the bunch of roses. He walks to and fro*] To judge by all signs, Summer is gone and Fall has come. The linden shows it, and the monk's-hood also. [*Walks*] But the Fall is *my* Spring, for then the opera begins again, and then she must come. Please, madam, may I sit down a little on this chair?

THE DAUGHTER. Yes, sit down, friend— I am able to stand.

THE OFFICER. [*Sits down*] If I could only get some sleep, then I should feel better—[*He falls asleep for a few moments. Then he jumps up and walks back and forth again. Stops at last in front of the door with the clover leaf and pokes at it*] This door here will not leave me any peace—what is behind it? There must be something. [*Faint dance music is heard from above*] Oh, now the rehearsals have begun. [*The light goes out and flares up again, repeating this rhythmically as the rays of a lighthouse come and go*] What does this mean? [*Speaking in time with the blinkings of the light*] Light and dark—light and dark?

THE DAUGHTER. [*Imitating him*] Night and day—night and day! A merciful Providence wants to shorten your wait. Therefore the days are flying in hot pursuit of the nights.

The light shines unbrokenly once more.

THE BILLPOSTER *enters with his dipnet and his implements.*

THE OFFICER. There is the Billposter with his dipnet. Was the fishing good?

THE BILLPOSTER. I should say so. The Summer was hot and a little long—the net turned out pretty good, but not as I had expected.

THE OFFICER. [*With emphasis*] Not as I had expected!— That is well said. Nothing ever was as I expected it to be— because the thought is more than the deed, more than the thing.

Walks to and fro, striking at the wall with the rose stems so that the last few leaves fall off.

THE BILLPOSTER. Has she not come down yet?

THE OFFICER. Not yet, but she will soon be here— Do you know what is behind that door, Billposter?

THE BILLPOSTER. No, I have never seen that door open yet.

THE OFFICER. I am going to telephone for a locksmith to come and open it.   [*Goes into the lodge.*

[THE BILLPOSTER *posts a bill and goes toward the right.*

THE DAUGHTER. What is the matter with the dipnet?

THE BILLPOSTER. Matter? Well, I don't know as there is anything the matter with it—but it just didn't turn out as I had expected, and the pleasure of it was not so much after all.

THE DAUGHTER. How did you expect it to be?

THE BILLPOSTER. How?— Well, I couldn't tell exactly——

THE DAUGHTER. I can tell you! You had expected it to be what it was not. It had to be green, but not that kind of green.

THE BILLPOSTER. You have it, madam. You understand it all—and that is why everybody goes to you with his worries. If you would only listen to me a little also——

THE DAUGHTER. Of course, I will!— Come in to me and pour out your heart.   [*She goes into the lodge.*

  [THE BILLPOSTER *remains outside, speaking to her. The stage is darkened again. When the light is turned on, the tree has resumed its leaves, the monk's-hood is blooming once more, and the sun is shining on the green space beyond the passageway.*

  THE OFFICER *enters. Now he is old and white-haired, ragged, and wearing worn-out shoes. He carries the bare remnants of the rose stems. Walks to and fro slowly, with the gait of an aged man. Reads on the posted bill.*

  A BALLET GIRL *comes in from the right.*

THE OFFICER. Is Miss Victoria gone?

THE BALLET GIRL. No, she has not gone yet.

THE OFFICER. Then I shall wait. She will be coming soon, don't you think?

THE BALLET GIRL. Oh, yes, I am sure.

THE OFFICER. Don't go away now, for I have sent word to the locksmith, so you will soon see what is behind that door.

THE BALLET GIRL. Oh, it will be awfully interesting to see that door opened. That door, there, and the Growing Castle—have you heard of the Growing Castle?

THE OFFICER. Have I?— I have been a prisoner in it.

THE BALLET GIRL. No, was that you? But why do they keep such a lot of horses there?

THE OFFICER. Because it is a stable castle, don't you know.

THE BALLET GIRL. [*With confusion*] How stupid of me not to guess that!

A MALE CHORUS SINGER *enters from the right.*

THE OFFICER. Has Miss Victoria gone yet?

THE CHORUS SINGER. [*Earnestly*] No, she has not. She never goes away.

THE OFFICER. That is because she loves me— See here, don't go before the locksmith comes to open the door here.

THE CHORUS SINGER. No, is the door going to be opened? Well, that will be fun!— I just want to ask the Portress something.

THE PROMPTER *enters from the right.*

THE OFFICER. Is Miss Victoria gone yet?

THE PROMPTER. Not that I know of.

THE OFFICER. Now, didn't I tell you she was waiting for me!— Don't go away, for the door is going to be opened.

THE PROMPTER. Which door?

THE OFFICER. Is there more than one door?

THE PROMPTER. Oh, I know—that one with the clover leaf. Well, then I have got to stay— I am only going to have a word with the Portress.

> THE BALLET GIRL, THE CHORUS SINGER, *and* THE PROMPTER *gather beside* THE BILLPOSTER *in front of the lodge window and talk by turns to* THE DAUGHTER.

THE GLAZIER *enters through the gate.*

THE OFFICER. Are you the locksmith?

THE GLAZIER. No, the locksmith had visitors, and a glazier will do just as well.

THE OFFICER. Yes, of course, of course—but did you bring your diamond along?

THE GLAZIER. Why, certainly!— A glazier without his diamond, what would that be?

THE OFFICER. Nothing at all!— Let us get to work then.

[*Claps his hands together.*

ALL *gather in a ring around the door.*

Male members of the chorus dressed as Master Singers and Ballet Girls in costumes from the opera "Aïda" enter from the right and join the rest.

THE OFFICER. Locksmith—or glazier—do your duty!

THE GLAZIER *goes up to the door with the diamond in his hand.*

THE OFFICER. A moment like this will not occur twice in a man's life. For this reason, my friends, I ask you—please consider carefully——

A POLICEMAN. [*Enters*] In the name of the law, I forbid the opening of that door!

THE OFFICER. Oh, Lord! What a fuss there is as soon as anybody wants to do anything new or great. But we will take the matter into court—let us go to the Lawyer. Then we shall see whether the laws still exist or not— Come along to the Lawyer.

Without lowering of the curtain, the stage changes to a lawyer's office, and in this manner. The gate remains, but as a wicket in the railing running clear across the stage. The gatekeeper's lodge turns into the private enclosure of the Lawyer, and it is now entirely open to the front. The linden, leafless, becomes a hat tree. The billboard is covered with legal notices and court decisions. The door with the four-leaved clover hole forms part of a document chest.

THE LAWYER, *in evening dress and white necktie, is found sitting to the left, inside the gate, and in front of him stands a desk covered with papers. His appearance indicates enormous sufferings. His face is chalk-white and full of wrinkles, and its shadows have a purple effect. He is ugly, and his features seem to reflect all the crimes and vices with which he has been forced by his profession to come into contact.*

Of his two clerks, one has lost an arm, the other an eye.

The people gathered to witness "the opening of the door" remain as before, but they appear now to be waiting for an audience with the Lawyer. Judging by their attitudes, one would think they had been standing there forever.

The Daughter, *still wearing the shawl, and* The Officer *are near the footlights.*

The Lawyer. [*Goes over to* The Daughter] Tell me, sister, can I have that shawl? I shall keep it here until I have a fire in my grate, and then I shall burn it with all its miseries and sorrows.

The Daughter. Not yet, brother. I want it to hold all it possibly can, and I want it above all to take up your agonies —all the confidences you have received about crime, vice, robbery, slander, abuse——

The Lawyer. My dear girl, for such a purpose your shawl would prove totally insufficient. Look at these walls. Does it not look as if the wall-paper itself had been soiled by every conceivable sin? Look at these documents into which I write tales of wrong. Look at myself— No smiling man ever comes here; nothing is to be seen here but angry glances, snarling lips, clenched fists— And everybody pours his anger, his envy, his suspicions, upon me. Look—my hands are black, and no washing will clean them. See how they are chapped and bleeding— I can never wear my clothes more than a few days because they smell of other people's crimes—

At times I have the place fumigated with sulphur, but it does not help. I sleep near by, and I dream of nothing but crimes— Just now I have a murder case in court—oh, I can stand that, but do you know what is worse than anything else?— That is to separate married people! Then it is as if something cried way down in the earth and up there in the sky—as if it cried treason against the primal force, against the source of all good, against love— And do you know, when reams of paper have been filled with mutual accusations, and at last a sympathetic person takes one of the two apart and asks, with a pinch of the ear or a smile, the simple question: what have you really got against your husband?—or your wife?—then he, or she, stands perplexed and cannot give the cause. Once—well, I think a lettuce salad was the principal issue; another time it was just a word—mostly it is nothing at all. But the tortures, the sufferings—these I have to bear— See how I look! Do you think I could ever win a woman's love with this countenance so like a criminal's? Do you think anybody dares to be friendly with me, who has to collect all the debts, all the money obligations, of the whole city?— It is a misery to be man!

THE DAUGHTER. Men are to be pitied!

THE LAWYER. They are. And what people are living on puzzles me. They marry on an income of two thousand, when they need four thousand. They borrow, of course— everybody borrows. In some sort of happy-go-lucky fashion, by the skin of their teeth, they manage to pull through—and thus it continues to the end, when the estate is found to be bankrupt. Who pays for it at last no one can tell.

THE DAUGHTER. Perhaps He who feeds the birds.

THE LAWYER. Perhaps. But if He who feeds the birds would only pay a visit to this earth of His and see for Himself how the poor human creatures fare—then His heart would surely fill with compassion.

THE DAUGHTER. Men are to be pitied!

THE LAWYER. Yes, that is the truth!— [*To* THE OFFICER] What do you want?

THE OFFICER. I just wanted to ask if Miss Victoria has gone yet.

THE LAWYER. No, she has not; you can be sure of it— Why are you poking at my chest over there?

THE OFFICER. I thought the door of it looked exactly——

THE LAWYER. Not at all! Not at all!

All the church bells begin to ring.

THE OFFICER. Is there going to be a funeral?

THE LAWYER. No, it is graduation day—a number of degrees will be conferred, and I am going to be made a Doctor of Laws. Perhaps you would also like to be graduated and receive a laurel wreath?

THE OFFICER. Yes, why not. That would be a diversion, at least.

THE LAWYER. Perhaps then we may begin upon this solemn function at once— But you had better go home and change your clothes.

[THE OFFICER *goes out.*

The stage is darkened and the following changes are made. The railing stays, but it encloses now the chancel of a church. The billboard displays hymn numbers. The linden hat tree becomes a candelabrum. The Lawyer's desk is turned into the desk of the presiding functionary, and the door with the clover leaf leads to the vestry.

The chorus of Master Singers become heralds with staffs, and the Ballet Girls carry laurel wreaths. The rest of the people act as spectators.

The background is raised, and the new one thus discovered represents a large church organ, with the keyboards below and the organist's mirror above.

Music is heard. At the sides stand figures symbolising the four academic faculties: Philosophy, Theology, Medicine, and Jurisprudence.

At first the stage is empty for a few moments.

  HERALDS *enter from the right.*

  BALLET GIRLS *follow with laurel wreaths carried high before them.*

  THREE GRADUATES *appear one after another from the left, receive their wreaths from the* BALLET GIRLS, *and go out to the right.*

  THE LAWYER *steps forward to get his wreath.*

  THE BALLET GIRLS *turn away from him and refuse to place the wreath on his head. Then they withdraw from the stage.*

  THE LAWYER, *shocked, leans against a column. All the others withdraw gradually until only* THE LAWYER *remains on the stage.*

THE DAUGHTER. [*Enters, her head and shoulders covered by a white veil*] Do you see, I have washed the shawl! But why are you standing there? Did you get your wreath?

THE LAWYER. No, I was not held worthy.

THE DAUGHTER. Why? Because you have defended the poor, put in a good word for the wrong-doing, made the burden easier for the guilty, obtained a respite for the condemned? Woe upon men: they are not angels—but they are to be pitied!

THE LAWYER. Say nothing evil of men—for after all it is my task to voice their side.

THE DAUGHTER. [*Leaning against the organ*] Why do they strike their friends in the face?

THE LAWYER. They know no better.

THE DAUGHTER. Let us enlighten them. Will you try? Together with me?

THE LAWYER. They do not accept enlightenment— Oh, that our plaint might reach the gods of heaven!

THE DAUGHTER. It shall reach the throne— [*Turns toward the organ*] Do you know what I see in this mirror?— The world turned the right way!— Yes indeed, for naturally we see it upside down.

THE LAWYER. How did it come to be turned the wrong way?

THE DAUGHTER. When the copy was taken——

THE LAWYER. You have said it! The copy— I have always had the feeling that it was a spoiled copy. And when I began to recall the original images, I grew dissatisfied with everything. But men called it soreheadedness, looking at the world through the devil's eyes, and other such things.

THE DAUGHTER. It is certainly a crazy world! Look at the four faculties here. The government, to which has fallen the task of preserving society, supports all four of them. Theology, the science of God, is constantly attacked and ridiculed by philosophy, which declares itself to be the sum of all wisdom. And medicine is always challenging philosophy, while refusing entirely to count theology a science and even insisting on calling it a mere superstition. And they belong to a common Academic Council, which has been set to teach the young respect—for the university. It is a bedlam. And woe unto him who first recovers his reason!

THE LAWYER. Those who find it out first are the theologians. As a preparatory study, they take philosophy, which teaches them that theology is nonsense. Later they learn from theology that philosophy is nonsense. Madmen, I should say!

THE DAUGHTER. And then there is jurisprudence which serves all but the servants.

THE LAWYER. Justice, which, when it wants to do right,

becomes the undoing of men. Equity, which so often turns into iniquity!

THE DAUGHTER. What a mess you have made of it, you man-children. Children, indeed!— Come here, and I will give you a wreath—one that is more becoming to you. [*Puts a crown of thorns on his head*] And now I will play for you.

> *She sits down at the keyboards, but instead of organ-notes human voices are heard.*

VOICES OF CHILDREN. O Lord everlasting!

> [*Last note sustained.*

VOICES OF WOMEN. Have mercy upon us!

> [*Last note sustained.*

VOICES OF MEN. [*Tenors*] Save us for Thy mercy's sake!

> [*Last note sustained.*

VOICES OF MEN. [*Basses*] Spare Thy children, O Lord, and deliver us from Thy wrath!

ALL. Have mercy upon us! Hear us! Have pity upon the mortals!— O Lord eternal, why art Thou afar?— Out of the depths we call unto Thee: Make not the burden of Thy children too heavy! Hear us! Hear us!

> *The stage turns dark.* THE DAUGHTER *rises and draws close to* THE LAWYER. *By a change of light, the organ becomes Fingal's Cave. The ground-swell of the ocean, which can be seen rising and falling between the columns of basalt, produces a deep harmony that blends the music of winds and waves.*

THE LAWYER. Where are we, sister?

THE DAUGHTER. What do you hear?

THE LAWYER. I hear drops falling——

THE DAUGHTER. Those are the tears that men are weeping— What more do you hear?

THE LAWYER. There is sighing—and whining—and wailing——

THE DAUGHTER. Hither the plaint of the mortals has reached—and no farther. But why this never-ending wailing? Is there then nothing in life to rejoice at?

THE LAWYER. Yes, what is most sweet, and what is also most bitter—love—wife and home—the highest and the lowest!

THE DAUGHTER. May I try it?

THE LAWYER. With me?

THE DAUGHTER. With you— You know the rocks, the stumbling-stones. Let us avoid them.

THE LAWYER. I am so poor.

THE DAUGHTER. What does that matter if we only love each other? And a little beauty costs nothing.

THE LAWYER. I have dislikes which may prove your likes.

THE DAUGHTER. They can be adjusted.

THE LAWYER. And if we tire of it?

THE DAUGHTER. Then come the children and bring with them a diversion that remains for ever new.

THE LAWYER. You, you will take me, poor and ugly, scorned and rejected?

THE DAUGHTER. Yes—let us unite our destinies.

THE LAWYER. So be it then!

Curtain.

An extremely plain room inside THE LAWYER's *office. To the right, a big double bed covered by a canopy and curtained in. Next to it, a window. To the left, an iron heater with cooking utensils on top of it.* CHRISTINE *is pasting paper strips along the cracks of the double windows. In the background, an open door to the office. Through the door are visible a number of poor clients waiting for admission.*

CHRISTINE. I paste, I paste.

THE DAUGHTER. [*Pale and emaciated, sits by the stove*] You shut out all the air. I choke!

CHRISTINE. Now there is only one little crack left.

THE DAUGHTER. Air, air—I cannot breathe!

CHRISTINE. I paste, I paste.

THE LAWYER. That's right, Christine! Heat is expensive.

THE DAUGHTER. Oh, it feels as if my lips were being glued together.

THE LAWYER. [*Standing in the doorway, with a paper in his hand*] Is the child asleep?

THE DAUGHTER. Yes, at last.

THE LAWYER. [*Gently*] All this crying scares away my clients.

THE DAUGHTER. [*Pleasantly*] What can be done about it?

THE LAWYER. Nothing.

THE DAUGHTER. We shall have to get a larger place.

THE LAWYER. We have no money for it.

THE DAUGHTER. May I open the window—this bad air is suffocating.

THE LAWYER. Then the heat escapes, and we shall be cold.

THE DAUGHTER. It is horrible!— May we clean up out there?

THE LAWYER. You have not the strength to do any cleaning, nor have I, and Christine must paste. She must put strips through the whole house, on every crack, in the ceiling, in the floor, in the walls.

THE DAUGHTER. Poverty I was prepared for, but not for dirt.

THE LAWYER. Poverty is always dirty, relatively speaking.

THE DAUGHTER. This is worse than I dreamed!

THE LAWYER. We are not the worst off by far. There is still food in the pot.

THE DAUGHTER. But what sort of food?

THE LAWYER. Cabbage is cheap, nourishing, and good to eat.

THE DAUGHTER. For those who like cabbage—to me it is repulsive.

THE LAWYER. Why didn't you say so?

THE DAUGHTER. Because I loved you, I wanted to sacrifice my own taste.

THE LAWYER. Then I must sacrifice my taste for cabbage to you—for sacrifices must be mutual.

THE DAUGHTER. What are we to eat, then? Fish? But you hate fish?

THE LAWYER. And it is expensive.

THE DAUGHTER. This is worse than I thought it!

THE LAWYER. [Kindly] Yes, you see how hard it is— And the child that was to become a link and a blessing—it becomes our ruin.

THE DAUGHTER. Dearest, I die in this air, in this room, with its backyard view, with its baby cries and endless hours of sleeplessness, with those people out there, and their whinings, and bickerings, and incriminations— I shall die here!

THE LAWYER. My poor little flower, that has no light and no air——

THE DAUGHTER. And you say that people exist who are still worse off?

THE LAWYER. I belong with the envied ones in this locality.

THE DAUGHTER. Everything else might be borne if I could only have some beauty in my home.

THE LAWYER. I know you are thinking of flowers—and especially of heliotropes—but a plant costs half a dollar, which will buy us six quarts of milk or a peck of potatoes.

THE DAUGHTER. I could gladly get along without food if I could only have some flowers.

THE LAWYER. There is a kind of beauty that costs nothing —but the absence of it in the home is worse than any other torture to a man with a sense for the beautiful.

THE DAUGHTER. What is it?

THE LAWYER. If I tell, you will get angry.

THE DAUGHTER. We have agreed not to get angry.

THE LAWYER. We have agreed—— Everything can be overcome, Agnes, except the short, sharp accents—— Do you know them? Not yet!

THE DAUGHTER. They will never be heard between us.

THE LAWYER. Not as far as it lies on me!

THE DAUGHTER. Tell me now.

THE LAWYER. Well—when I come into a room, I look first of all at the curtains—[Goes over to the window and straightens out the curtains] If they hang like ropes or rags, then I leave soon. And next I take a glance at the chairs—if they stand straight along the wall, then I stay. [Puts a chair back against the wall] Finally I look at the candles in their sticks— if they point this way and that, then the whole house is askew.

[*Straightens up a candle on the chest of drawers*] This is the kind of beauty, dear heart, that costs nothing.

THE DAUGHTER. [*With bent head*] Beware of the short accents, Axel!

THE LAWYER. They were not short.

THE DAUGHTER. Yes, they were.

THE LAWYER. Well, I'll be——

THE DAUGHTER. What kind of language is that?

THE LAWYER. Pardon me, Agnes! But I have suffered as much from your lack of orderliness as you have suffered from dirt. And I have not dared to set things right myself, for when I do so, you get as angry as if I were reproaching you—ugh! Hadn't we better quit now?

THE DAUGHTER. It is very difficult to be married—it is more difficult than anything else. One has to be an angel, I think!

THE LAWYER. I think so, too.

THE DAUGHTER. I fear I shall begin to hate you after this!

THE LAWYER. Woe to us then!— But let us forestall hatred. I promise never again to speak of any untidiness—although it is torture to me!

THE DAUGHTER. And I shall eat cabbage though it means agony to me.

THE LAWYER. A life of common suffering, then! One's pleasure, the other one's pain!

THE DAUGHTER. Men are to be pitied!

THE LAWYER. You see that?

THE DAUGHTER. Yes, but for heaven's sake, let us avoid the rocks, now when we know them so well.

THE LAWYER. Let us try! Are we not decent and intelligent persons? Able to forbear and forgive?

THE DAUGHTER. Why not smile at mere trifles?

THE LAWYER. We—only we—can do so. Do you know, I read this morning—by the bye, where is the newspaper?

THE DAUGHTER. [*Embarrassed*] Which newspaper?

THE LAWYER. [*Sharply*] Do I keep more than one?

THE DAUGHTER. Smile now, and don't speak sharply— I used your paper to make the fire with——

THE LAWYER. [*Violently*] Well, I'll be damned!

THE DAUGHTER. Why don't you smile?— I burned it because it ridiculed what is holy to me.

THE LAWYER. Which is unholy to me! Yah! [*Strikes one clenched fist against the open palm of the other hand*] I smile, I smile so that my wisdom teeth show— Of course, I am to be nice, and I am to swallow my own opinions, and say yes to everything, and cringe and dissemble! [*Tidies the curtains around the bed*] That's it! Now I am going to fix things until you get angry again— Agnes, this is simply impossible!

THE DAUGHTER. Of course it is!

THE LAWYER. And yet we must endure—not for the sake of our promises, but for the sake of the child!

THE DAUGHTER. You are right—for the sake of the child. Oh, oh—we have to endure!

THE LAWYER. And now I must go out to my clients. Listen to them—how they growl with impatience to tear each other, to get each other fined and jailed— Lost souls!

THE DAUGHTER. Poor, poor people! And this pasting!

[*She drops her head forward in dumb despair.*

CHRISTINE. I paste, I paste.

THE LAWYER *stands at the door, twisting the door-knob nervously.*

THE DAUGHTER. How that knob squeaks! It is as if you were twisting my heart-strings——

THE LAWYER. I twist, I twist!

THE DAUGHTER. Don't!

THE LAWYER. I twist!

THE DAUGHTER. No!

THE LAWYER. I——

THE OFFICER. [*In the office, on the other side of the door, takes hold of the knob*] Will you permit me?

THE LAWYER. [*Lets go his hold*] By all means. Seeing that you have your degree!

THE OFFICER. Now all life belongs to me. Every road lies open. I have mounted Parnassus. The laurel is won. Immortality, fame, all is mine!

THE LAWYER. And what are you going to live on?

THE OFFICER. Live on?

THE LAWYER. You must have a home, clothes, food——

THE OFFICER. Oh, that will come—if you can only find somebody to love you!

THE LAWYER. You don't say so!— You don't— Paste, Christine, paste until they cannot breathe!

[*Goes out backward, nodding.*

CHRISTINE. I paste, I paste—until they cannot breathe.

THE OFFICER. Will you come with me now?

THE DAUGHTER. At once! But where?

THE OFFICER. To Fairhaven. There it is summer; there the sun is shining; there we find youth, children, and flowers, singing and dancing, feasting and frolicking.

THE DAUGHTER. Then I will go there.

THE OFFICER. Come!

THE LAWYER. [*Enters again*] Now I go back to my first hell—this was the second and greater. The sweeter the hell, the greater— And look here, now she has been dropping hair-pins on the floor again. [*He picks up some hair-pins.*

THE OFFICER. My! but he has discovered the pins also.

THE LAWYER. Also?— Look at this one. You see two prongs, but it is only one pin. It is two, yet only one. If I

bend it open, it is a single piece. If I bend it back, there are
two, but they remain one for all that. It means: these two
are one. But if I break—like this!—then they become two.

[*Breaks the pin and throws the pieces away.*

THE OFFICER. All that he has seen!— But before break-
ing, the prongs must diverge. If they point together, then it
holds.

THE LAWYER. And if they are parallel, then they will
never meet—and it neither breaks nor holds.

THE OFFICER. The hair-pin is the most perfect of all created
things. A straight line which equals two parallel ones.

THE LAWYER. A lock that shuts when it is open.

THE OFFICER. And thus shuts in a braid of hair that opens
up when the lock shuts.

THE LAWYER. It is like this door. When I close it, then
I open—the way out—for you, Agnes!

[*Withdraws and closes the door behind him.*

THE DAUGHTER. Well then ?

*The stage changes. The bed with its curtains becomes a tent.
The stove stays as it was. The background is raised.*

*To the right, in the foreground, are seen hills stripped of their
trees by fire, and red heather growing between the blackened
tree stumps. Red-painted pig-sties and outhouses. Beyond these, in the open, apparatus for mechanical gymnas-
tics, where sick persons are being treated on machines resembling instruments of torture.*

*To the left, in the foreground, the quarantine station, consisting
of open sheds, with ovens, furnaces, and pipe coils.*

In the middle distance, a narrow strait.

*The background shows a beautiful wooded shore. Flags are
flying on its piers, where ride white sailboats, some with
sails set and some without. Little Italian villas, pavilions,*

arbors, marble statues are glimpsed through the foliage along the shore.

THE MASTER OF QUARANTINE, *made up like a blacka-moor, is walking along the shore.*

THE OFFICER. [*Meets him and they shake hands*] Why, Ordström![1] Have you landed here?

MASTER OF Q. Yes, here I am.

THE OFFICER. Is this Fairhaven?

MASTER OF Q. No, that is on the other side. This is Foulstrand.

THE OFFICER. Then we have lost our way.

MASTER OF Q. We?— Won't you introduce me?

THE OFFICER. No, that wouldn't do. [*In a lowered voice*] It is Indra's own daughter.

MASTER OF Q. Indra's? And I was thinking of Varuna himself— Well, are you not surprised to find me black in the face?

THE OFFICER. I am past fifty, my boy, and at that age one has ceased to be surprised. I concluded at once that you were bound for some fancy ball this afternoon.

MASTER OF Q. Right you were! And I hope both of you will come along.

THE OFFICER. Why, yes—for I must say—the place does not look very tempting. What kind of people live here any-how?

MASTER OF Q. Here you find the sick; over there, the healthy.

THE OFFICER. Nothing but poor folk on this side, I sup-pose.

MASTER OF Q. No, my boy, it is here you find the rich. Look at that one on the rack. He has stuffed himself with

---

[1] Means literally "wordspout."

paté de foie gras and truffles and Burgundy until his feet have grown knotted.

THE OFFICER. Knotted?

MASTER OF Q. Yes, he has a case of knotted feet.   And that one who lies under the guillotine—he has swilled brandy so that his backbone has to be put through the mangle.

THE OFFICER. There is always something amiss!

MASTER OF Q. Moreover, everybody living on this side has some kind of canker to hide.   Look at the fellow coming here, for instance.

> *An old dandy is pushed on the stage in a wheel-chair.*
> *He is accompanied by a gaunt and grisly coquette in*
> *the sixties, to whom* THE FRIEND, *a man of about*
> *forty, is paying court.*

THE OFFICER. It is the major—our schoolmate!

MASTER OF Q. Don Juan.   Can you see that he is still enamored of that old spectre beside him?   He does not notice that she has grown old, or that she is ugly, faithless, cruel.

THE OFFICER. Why, that is love!   And I couldn't have dreamt that a fickle fellow like him would prove capable of loving so deeply and so earnestly.

MASTER OF Q. That is a mighty decent way of looking at it.

THE OFFICER. I have been in love with Victoria myself— in fact I am still waiting for her in the passageway——

MASTER OF Q. Oh, you are the fellow who is waiting in the passageway?

THE OFFICER. I am the man.

MASTER OF Q. Well, have you got that door opened yet?

THE OFFICER. No, the case is still in court— The Bill-poster is out with his dipnet, of course, so that the taking of evidence is always being put off—and in the meantime the Glazier has mended all the window panes in the castle, which has grown half a story higher— This has been an uncommonly good year—warm and wet——

MASTER OF Q. But just the same you have had no heat comparing with what I have here.

THE OFFICER. How much do you have in your ovens?

MASTER OF Q. When we fumigate cholera suspects, we run it up to one hundred and forty degrees.

THE OFFICER. Is the cholera going again?

MASTER OF Q. Don't you know that?

THE OFFICER. Of course, I know it, but I forget so often what I know.

MASTER OF Q. I wish often that I could forget—especially myself. That is why I go in for masquerades and carnivals and amateur theatricals.

THE OFFICER. What have you been up to then?

MASTER OF Q. If I told, they would say that I was boasting; and if I don't tell, then they call me a hypocrite.

THE OFFICER. That is why you blackened your face?

MASTER OF Q. Exactly—making myself a shade blacker than I am.

THE OFFICER. Who is coming there?

MASTER OF Q. Oh, a poet who is going to have his mud bath.

> THE POET *enters with his eyes raised toward the sky and carrying a pail of mud in one hand.*

THE OFFICER. Why, he ought to be having light baths and air baths.

MASTER OF Q. No, he is roaming about the higher regions so much that he gets homesick for the mud—and wallowing in the mire makes the skin callous like that of a pig. Then he cannot feel the stings of the wasps.

THE OFFICER. This is a queer world, full of contradictions.

THE POET. [*Ecstatically*] Man was created by the god

Phtah out of clay on a potter's wheel, or a lathe—[*sceptically*], or any damned old thing! [*Ecstatically*] Out of clay does the sculptor create his more or less immortal masterpieces— [*sceptically*], which mostly are pure rot. [*Ecstatically*] Out of clay they make those utensils which are so indispensable in the pantry and which generically are named pots and plates— [*sceptically*], but what in thunder does it matter to me what they are called anyhow? [*Ecstatically*] Such is the clay! When clay becomes fluid, it is called mud— C'est mon affaire!— [*shouts*] Lena!

LENA *enters with a pail in her hand.*

THE POET. Lena, show yourself to Miss Agnes— She knew you ten years ago, when you were a young, happy and, let us say, pretty girl— Behold how she looks now. Five children, drudgery, baby-cries, hunger, ill-treatment. See how beauty has perished and joy vanished in the fulfilment of duties which should have brought that inner satisfaction which makes each line in the face harmonious and fills the eye with a quiet glow.

MASTER OF Q. [*Covering the poet's mouth with his hand*] Shut up! Shut up!

THE POET. That is what they all say. And if you keep silent, then they cry: speak! Oh, restless humanity!

THE DAUGHTER. [*Goes to* LENA] Tell me your troubles.

LENA. No, I dare not, for then they will be made worse.

THE DAUGHTER. Who could be so cruel?

LENA. I dare not tell, for if I do, I shall be spanked.

THE POET. That is just what will happen. But I will speak, even though the blackamoor knock out all my teeth— I will tell that justice is not always done— Agnes, daughter of the gods, do you hear music and dancing on the hill over there?— Well, it is Lena's sister who has come home from the city where she went astray—you understand? Now they are killing the fatted calf; but Lena, who stayed at home, has to carry slop pails and feed the pigs.

THE DAUGHTER. There is rejoicing at home because the stray has left the paths of evil, and not merely because she has come back. Bear that in mind.

THE POET. But then they should give a ball and banquet every night for the spotless worker that never strayed into paths of error— Yet they do nothing of the kind, but when Lena has a free moment, she is sent to prayer-meetings where she has to hear reproaches for not being perfect. Is this justice?

THE DAUGHTER. Your question is so difficult to answer because— There are so many unforeseen cases——

THE POET. That much the Caliph, Haroun the Just, came to understand. He was sitting on his throne, and from its height he could never make out what happened below. At last complaints penetrated to his exalted ears. And then, one fine day, he disguised himself and descended unobserved among the crowds to find out what kind of justice they were getting.

THE DAUGHTER. I hope you don't take me for Haroun the Just!

THE OFFICER. Let us talk of something else— Here come visitors.

> A white boat, shaped like a viking ship, with a dragon for figure-head, with a pale-blue silken sail on a gilded yard, and with a rose-red standard flying from the top of a gilded mast, glides through the strait from the left. HE and SHE are seated in the stern with their arms around each other.

THE OFFICER. Behold perfect happiness, bliss without limits, young love's rejoicing!

> The stage grows brighter.

HE. [*Stands up in the boat and sings*]

> Hail, beautiful haven,
> Where the Springs of my youth were spent,
> Where my first sweet dreams were dreamt—
> To thee I return,
> But lonely no longer!

> Ye hills and groves,
> Thou sky o'erhead,
> Thou mirroring sea,
> Give greeting to her:
> My love, my bride,
> My light and my life!

> *The flags at the landings of Fairhaven are dipped in*
> *salute; white handkerchiefs are waved from veran-*
> *dahs and boats, and the air is filled with tender chords*
> *from harps and violins.*

THE POET. See the light that surrounds them!   Hear how
the air is ringing with music!—   Eros!

THE OFFICER. It is Victoria.

MASTER OF Q. Well, what of it?

The OFFICER. It is his Victoria—   My own is still mine.
And nobody can see *her*—   Now you hoist the quarantine
flag, and I shall pull in the net.

> [THE MASTER OF QUARANTINE *waves a yellow flag.*

THE OFFICER. [*Pulling a rope that turns the boat toward*
Foulstrand] Hold on there!

> HE *and* SHE *become aware of the hideous view and give*
> *vent to their horror.*

MASTER OF Q. Yes, it comes hard.   But here every one
must stop who hails from plague-stricken places.

THE POET. The idea of speaking in such manner, of acting in such a way, within the presence of two human beings

united in love! Touch them not! Lay not hands on love!
It is treason!— Woe to us! Everything beautiful must now
be dragged down—dragged into the mud!

[HE *and* SHE *step ashore, looking sad and shamefaced.*

HE. Woe to us! What have we done?

MASTER OF Q. It is not necessary to have done anything
in order to encounter life's little pricks.

SHE. So short-lived are joy and happiness!

HE. How long must we stay here?

MASTER OF Q. Forty days and nights.

SHE. Then rather into the water!

HE. To live here—among blackened hills and pig-sties?

THE POET. Love overcomes all, even sulphur fumes and
carbolic acid.

MASTER OF Q. [*Starts a fire in the store: blue, sulphurous
flames break forth*] Now I set the sulphur going. Will you
please step in?

SHE. Oh, my blue dress will fade.

MASTER OF Q. And become white. So your roses will
also turn white in time.

HE. Even your cheeks—in forty days!

SHE. [*To* THE OFFICER] That will please you.

THE OFFICER. No, it will not!— Of course, your happiness was the cause of my suffering, but—it doesn't matter—
for I am graduated and have obtained a position over there
—heigh-ho and alas! And in the Fall I shall be teaching
school—teaching boys the same lessons I myself learned during my childhood and youth—the same lessons throughout
my manhood and, finally, in my old age—the self-same lessons! What does twice two make? How many times can
four be evenly divided by two?— Until I get a pension and
can do nothing at all—just wait around for meals and the
newspapers—until at last I am carted to the crematorium

and burned to ashes— Have you nobody here who is entitled
to a pension? Barring twice two makes four, it is probably
the worst thing of all—to begin school all over again when one
already is graduated; to ask the same questions until death
comes——

    *An elderly man goes by, with his hands folded behind
    his back.*

THE OFFICER. There is a pensioner now, waiting for himself to die. I think he must be a captain who missed the rank
of major; or an assistant judge who was not made a chief
justice. Many are called but few are chosen— He is waiting for his breakfast now.

THE PENSIONER. No, for the newspaper—the morning
paper.

THE OFFICER. And he is only fifty-four years old. He
may spend twenty-five more years waiting for meals and
newspapers—is it not dreadful?

THE PENSIONER. What is not dreadful? Tell me, tell me!

THE OFFICER. Tell that who can!— Now I shall have
to teach boys that twice two makes four. And how many
times four can be evenly divided by two. [*He clutches his head
in despair*] And Victoria, whom I loved and therefore wished
all the happiness life can give—now she has her happiness,
the greatest one known to her, and for this reason I suffer—
suffer, suffer!

SHE. Do you think I can be happy when I see you suffering?
How can you think it? Perhaps it will soothe your pains that
I am to be imprisoned here for forty days and nights? Tell
me, does it soothe your pains?

THE OFFICER. Yes and no. How can I enjoy seeing you
suffer? Oh!

SHE. And do you think my happiness can be founded on
your torments?

THE OFFICER. We are to be pitied—all of us!

ALL. [*Raise their arms toward the sky and utter a cry of anguish that sounds like a dissonant chord*] Oh!

THE DAUGHTER. Everlasting One, hear them! Life is evil! Men are to be pitied!

ALL. [*As before*] Oh!

For a moment the stage is completely darkened, and during that moment everybody withdraws or takes up a new position. When the light is turned on again, Foulstrand is seen in the background, lying in deep shadow. The strait is in the middle distance and Fairhaven in the foreground, both steeped in light. To the right, a corner of the Casino, where dancing couples are visible through the open windows. Three servant maids are standing outside on top of an empty box, with arms around each other, staring at the dancers within. On the verandah of the Casino stands a bench, where "PLAIN" EDITH is sitting. She is bareheaded, with an abundance of tousled hair, and looks sad. In front of her is an open piano.

To the left, a frame house painted yellow. Two children in light dresses are playing ball outside.

In the centre of the middle distance, a pier with white sailboats tied to it, and flag poles with hoisted flags. In the strait is anchored a naval vessel, brig-rigged, with gun ports.

But the entire landscape is in winter dress, with snow on the ground and on the bare trees.

THE DAUGHTER *and* THE OFFICER *enter.*

THE DAUGHTER. Here is peace, and happiness, and leisure. No more toil; every day a holiday; everybody dressed up in their best; dancing and music in the early morning. [*To the maids*] Why don't you go in and have a dance, girls?

THE MAIDS. We?

THE OFFICER. They are servants, don't you see!

THE DAUGHTER. Of course!— But why is Edith sitting there instead of dancing?

[EDITH *buries her face in her hands.*

THE OFFICER. Don't question her! She has been sitting there three hours without being asked for a dance.

[*Goes into the yellow house on the left.*

THE DAUGHTER. What a cruel form of amusement!

THE MOTHER. [*In a low-necked dress, enters from the Casino and goes up to* EDITH] Why don't you go in as I told you?

EDITH. Because—I cannot throw myself at them. That I am ugly, I know, and I know that nobody wants to dance with me, but I might be spared from being reminded of it.

Begins to play on the piano, the Toccata Con Fuga, Op. 10, by Sebastian Bach.

The waltz music from within is heard faintly at first. Then it grows in strength, as if to compete with the Bach Toccata. EDITH *prevails over it and brings it to silence. Dancers appear in the doorway to hear her play. Everybody on the stage stands still and listens reverently.*

A NAVAL OFFICER. [*Takes* ALICE, *one of the dancers, around the waist and drags her toward the pier*] Come quick!

EDITH *breaks off abruptly, rises and stares at the couple with an expression of utter despair; stands as if turned to stone.*

*Now the front wall of the yellow house disappears, revealing
three benches full of schoolboys. Among these* The
Officer *is seen, looking worried and depressed. In front
of the boys stands* The Teacher, *bespectacled and holding
a piece of chalk in one hand, a rattan cane in the other.*

The Teacher. [*To* The Officer] Well, my boy, can you
tell me what twice two makes?

      The Officer *remains seated while he racks his mind
without finding an answer.*

The Teacher. You must rise when I ask you a question.

The Officer. [*Harassed, rises*] Two—twice—let me see.
That makes two-two.

The Teacher. I see! You have not studied your lesson.

The Officer. [*Ashamed*] Yes, I have, but—I know the
answer, but I cannot tell it——

The Teacher. You want to wriggle out of it, of course.
You know it, but you cannot tell. Perhaps I may help you.
                              [*Pulls his hair.*

The Officer. Oh, it is dreadful, it is dreadful!

The Teacher. Yes, it is dreadful that such a big boy lacks
all ambition——

The Officer. [*Hurt*] Big boy—yes, I am big—bigger than
all these others—I am full-grown, I am done with school—
[*As if waking up*] I have graduated—why am I then sitting
here? Have I not received my doctor's degree?

The Teacher. Certainly, but you are to sit here and
mature, you know. You have to mature—isn't that so?

The Officer. [*Feels his forehead*] Yes, that is right, one
must mature— Twice two—makes two—and this I can de-
monstrate by analogy, which is the highest form of all rea-
soning. Listen!— Once one makes one; consequently twice
two must make two. For what applies in one case must also
apply in another.

THE TEACHER. Your conclusion is based on good logic, but your answer is wrong.

THE OFFICER. What is logical cannot be wrong. Let us test it. One divided by one gives one, so that two divided by two must give two.

THE TEACHER. Correct according to analogy. But how much does once three make?

THE OFFICER. Three, of course.

THE TEACHER. Consequently twice three must also make three.

THE OFFICER. [*Pondering*] No, that cannot be right—it cannot—or else— [*Sits down dejectedly*] No, I am not mature yet.

THE TEACHER. No, indeed, you are far from mature.

THE OFFICER. But how long am I to sit here, then?

THE TEACHER. Here—how 'long? Do you believe that time and space exist?— Suppose that time does exist, then you should be able to say what time is. What is time?

THE OFFICER. Time— [*Thinks*] I cannot tell, but I know what it is. Consequently I may also know what twice two is without being able to tell it. And, teacher, can you tell what time is?

THE TEACHER. Of course I can.

ALL THE BOYS. Tell us then!

THE TEACHER. Time—let me see. [*Stands immovable with one finger on his nose*] While we are talking, time flies. Consequently time is something that flies while we talk.

A BOY. [*Rising*] Now you are talking, teacher, and while you are talking, I fly: consequently I am time. [*Runs out.*

THE TEACHER. That accords completely with the laws of logic.

THE OFFICER. Then the laws of logic are silly, for Nils who ran away, cannot be time.

THE TEACHER. That is also good logic, although it is silly.

THE OFFICER. Then logic itself is silly.

THE TEACHER. So it seems. But if logic is silly, then all the world is silly—and then the devil himself wouldn't stay here to teach you more silliness. If anybody treats me to a drink, we'll go and take a bath.

THE OFFICER. That is a *posterus prius*, or the world turned upside down, for it is customary to bathe first and have the drink afterward. Old fogy!

THE TEACHER. Beware of a swelled head, doctor!

THE OFFICER. Call me captain, if you please. I am an officer, and I cannot understand why I should be sitting here to get scolded like a schoolboy——

THE TEACHER. [*With raised index finger*] We were to mature!

MASTER OF Q. [*Enters*] The quarantine begins.

THE OFFICER. Oh, there you are. Just think of it, this fellow makes me sit among the boys although I am graduated.

MASTER OF Q. Well, why don't you go away?

THE OFFICER. Heaven knows!— Go away? Why, that is no easy thing to do.

THE TEACHER. I guess not—just try!

THE OFFICER. [*To* MASTER OF QUARANTINE] Save me! Save me from his eye!

MASTER OF Q. Come on. Come and help us dance— We have to dance before the plague breaks out. We must!

THE OFFICER. Is the brig leaving?

MASTER OF Q. Yes, first of all the brig must leave— Then there will be a lot of tears shed, of course.

THE OFFICER. Always tears: when she comes and when she goes— Let us get out of here.

> *They go out.* THE TEACHER *continues his lesson in silence.*

THE MAIDS *that were staring through the window of the dance hall walk sadly down to the pier.* EDITH, *who has been standing like a statue at the piano, follows them.*

THE DAUGHTER. [*To* THE OFFICER] Is there not one happy person to be found in this paradise?

THE OFFICER. Yes, there is a newly married couple. Just watch them.

THE NEWLY MARRIED COUPLE *enter.*

HUSBAND. [*To his* WIFE] My joy has no limits, and I could now wish to die——

WIFE. Why die?

HUSBAND. Because at the heart of happiness grows the seed of disaster. Happiness devours itself like a flame—it cannot burn for ever, but must go out some time. And this presentiment of the coming end destroys joy in the very hour of its culmination.

WIFE. Let us then die together—this moment!

HUSBAND. Die? All right! For I fear happiness—that cheat! [*They go toward the water.*

THE DAUGHTER. Life is evil! Men are to be pitied!

THE OFFICER. Look at this fellow. He is the most envied mortal in this neighbourhood.

THE BLIND MAN *is led in.*

THE OFFICER. He is the owner of these hundred or more Italian villas. He owns all these bays, straits, shores, forests, together with the fishes in the water, the birds in the air, the game in the woods. These thousand or more people are his tenants. The sun rises upon his sea and sets upon his land——

THE DAUGHTER. Well—is he complaining also?

THE OFFICER. Yes, and with right, for he cannot see.

MASTER OF Q. He is blind.

THE DAUGHTER. The most envied of all!

THE OFFICER. Now he has come to see the brig depart
with his son on board.

THE BLIND MAN. I cannot see, but I hear. I hear the
anchor bill claw the clay bottom as when the hook is torn out
of a fish and brings up the heart with it through the neck—
My son, my only child, is going to journey across the wide
sea to foreign lands, and I can follow him only in my thought!
Now I hear the clanking of the chain—and—there is something that snaps and cracks like clothes drying on a line—
wet handkerchiefs perhaps. And I hear it blubber and snivel
as when people are weeping—maybe the splashing of the
wavelets among the seines—or maybe girls along the shore,
deserted and disconsolate— Once I asked a child why the
ocean is salt, and the child, which had a father on a long trip
across the high seas, said immediately: the ocean is salt because the sailors shed so many tears into it. And why do the
sailors cry so much then?— Because they are always going
away, replied the child; and that is why they are always drying their handkerchiefs in the rigging— And why does man
weep when he is sad? I asked at last— Because the glass in
the eyes must be washed now and then, so that we can see
clearly, said the child.

> *The brig has set sail and is gliding off. The girls along
> the shore are alternately waving their handkerchiefs
> and wiping off their tears with them. Then a signal
> is set on the foremast—a red ball in a white field, mean-
> ing "yes." In response to it* ALICE *waves her hand-
> kerchief triumphantly.*

THE DAUGHTER. [*To* THE OFFICER] What is the meaning of that flag?

THE OFFICER. It means "yes." It is the lieutenant's
troth—red as the red blood of the arteries, set against the blue
cloth of the sky.

THE DAUGHTER. And how does "no" look?

THE OFFICER. It is blue as the spoiled blood in the veins —but look, how jubilant Alice is.

THE DAUGHTER. And how Edith cries.

THE BLIND MAN. Meet and part.   Part and meet.   That is life.   I met his mother.   And then she went away from me. He was left to me; and now he goes.

THE DAUGHTER. But he will come back.

THE BLIND MAN. Who is speaking to me?   I have heard that voice before—in my dreams; in my youth, when vacation began; in the early years of my marriage, when my child was born.   Every time life smiled at me, I heard that voice, like a whisper of the south wind, like a chord of harps from above, like what I feel the angels' greeting must be in the Holy Night——

> THE LAWYER *enters and goes up to whisper something into* THE BLIND MAN's *ear.*

THE BLIND MAN. Is that so?

THE LAWYER. That's the truth. [*Goes to* THE DAUGHTER] Now you have seen most of it, but you have not yet tried the worst of it.

THE DAUGHTER. What can that be?

THE LAWYER. Repetition—recurrence.   To retrace one's own tracks; to be sent back to the task once finished—come!

THE DAUGHTER. Where?

THE LAWYER. To your duties.

THE DAUGHTER. What does that mean?

THE LAWYER. Everything you dread.   Everything you do not want but must.   It means to forego, to give up, to do without, to lack—it means everything that is unpleasant, repulsive, painful.

THE DAUGHTER. Are there no pleasant duties?

THE LAWYER. They become pleasant when they are done.

THE DAUGHTER. When they have ceased to exist— Duty is then something unpleasant. What is pleasant then?

THE LAWYER. What is pleasant is sin.

THE DAUGHTER. Sin?

THE LAWYER. Yes, something that has to be punished. If I have had a pleasant day or night, then I suffer infernal pangs and a bad conscience the next day.

THE DAUGHTER. How strange!

THE LAWYER. I wake up in the morning with a headache; and then the repetitions begin, but so that everything becomes perverted. What the night before was pretty, agreeable, witty, is presented by memory in the morning as ugly, distasteful, stupid. Pleasure seems to decay, and all joy goes to pieces. What men call success serves always as a basis for their next failure. My own successes have brought ruin upon me. For men view the fortune of others with an instinctive dread. They regard it unjust that fate should favour any one man, and so they try to restore balance by piling rocks on the road. To have talent is to be in danger of one's life, for then one may easily starve to death!— However, you will have to return to your duties, or I shall bring suit against you, and we shall pass through every court up to the highest—one, two, three!

THE DAUGHTER. Return?— To the iron stove, and the cabbage pot, and the baby clothes——

THE LAWYER. Exactly! We have a big wash to-day, for we must wash all the handkerchiefs——

THE DAUGHTER. Oh, must I do it all over again?

THE LAWYER. All life is nothing but doing things over again. Look at the teacher in there— He received his doctor's degree yesterday, was laurelled and saluted, climbed Parnassus and was embraced by the monarch—and to-day he starts school all over again, asks how much twice two makes.

and will continue to do so until his death— However, you must come back to your home!

THE DAUGHTER. I shall rather die!

THE LAWYER. Die?— That is not allowed. First of all, it is a disgrace—so much so that even the dead body is subjected to insults; and secondly, one goes to hell—it is a mortal sin!

THE DAUGHTER. It is not easy to be human!

ALL. Hear!

THE DAUGHTER. I shall not go back with you to humiliation and dirt— I am longing for the heights whence I came —but first the door must be opened so that I may learn the secret— It is my will that the door be opened!

THE LAWYER. Then you must retrace your own steps, cover the road you have already travelled, suffer all annoyances, repetitions, tautologies, recopyings, that a suit will bring with it——

THE DAUGHTER. May it come then— But first I must go into the solitude and the wilderness to recover my own self. We shall meet again! [*To* THE POET] Follow me.

> *Cries of anguish are heard from a distance.* Woe! Woe! Woe!

THE DAUGHTER. What is that?

THE LAWYER. The lost souls at Foulstrand.

THE DAUGHTER. Why do they wail more loudly than usual to-day?

THE LAWYER. Because the sun is shining here; because here we have music, dancing, youth. And it makes them feel their own sufferings more keenly.

THE DAUGHTER. We must set them free.

THE LAWYER. Try it! Once a liberator appeared, and he was nailed to a cross.

THE DAUGHTER. By whom?

THE LAWYER. By all the right-minded.

THE DAUGHTER. Who are they?

THE LAWYER. Are you not acquainted with all the right-minded? Then you must learn to know them.

THE DAUGHTER. Were they the ones that prevented your graduation?

THE LAWYER. Yes.

THE DAUGHTER. Then I know them!

Curtain.

*On the shores of the Mediterranean. To the left, in the fore-
ground, a white wall, and above it branches of an orange
tree with ripe fruit on them. In the background, villas
and a Casino placed on a terrace. To the right, a huge
pile of coal and two wheel-barrows. In the background, to
the right, a corner of blue sea.*

*Two coalheavers, naked to the waist, their faces, hands, and
bodies blackened by coal dust, are seated on the wheel-
barrows. Their expressions show intense despair.*

THE DAUGHTER *and* THE LAWYER *in the background.*

THE DAUGHTER. This is paradise!

FIRST COALHEAVER. This is hell!

SECOND COALHEAVER. One hundred and twenty degrees
in the shadow.

FIRST HEAVER. Let's have a bath.

SECOND HEAVER. The police won't let us. No bathing
here.

FIRST HEAVER. Couldn't we pick some fruit off that tree?

SECOND HEAVER. Then the police would get after us.

FIRST HEAVER. But I cannot do a thing in this heat— I'll
just chuck the job——

SECOND HEAVER. Then the police will get you for sure!—
[*Pause*] And you wouldn't have anything to eat anyhow.

FIRST HEAVER. Nothing to eat? We, who work hardest,
get least food; and the rich, who do nothing, get most. Might
one not—without disregard of truth—assert that this is injus-
tice?— What has the daughter of the gods to say about it?

THE DAUGHTER. I can say nothing at all— But tell me,

78

what have you done that makes you so black and your lot so hard?

FIRST HEAVER. What have we done? We have been born of poor and perhaps not very good parents— Maybe we have been punished a couple of times.

THE DAUGHTER. Punished?

FIRST HEAVER. Yes, the unpunished hang out in the Casino up there and dine on eight courses with wine.

THE DAUGHTER. [To THE LAWYER] Can that be true?

THE LAWYER. On the whole, yes.

THE DAUGHTER. You mean to say that every man at some time has deserved to go to prison?

THE LAWYER. Yes.

THE DAUGHTER. You, too?

THE LAWYER. Yes.

THE DAUGHTER. Is it true that the poor cannot bathe in the sea?

THE LAWYER. Yes. Not even with their clothes on. None but those who intend to take their own lives escape being fined. And those are said to get a good drubbing at the police station.

THE DAUGHTER. But can they not go outside of the city, out into the country, and bathe there?

THE LAWYER. There is no place for them—all the land is fenced in.

THE DAUGHTER. But I mean in the free, open country.

THE LAWYER. There is no such thing—it all belongs to somebody.

THE DAUGHTER. Even the sea, the great, vast sea——

THE LAWYER. Even that! You cannot sail the sea in a boat and land anywhere without having it put down in writing and charged for. It is lovely!

THE DAUGHTER. This is not paradise.

THE LAWYER. I should say not!

THE DAUGHTER. Why don't men do something to improve their lot?

THE LAWYER. Oh, they try, of course, but all the improvers end in prison or in the madhouse——

THE DAUGHTER. Who puts them in prison?

THE LAWYER. All the right-minded, all the respectable——

THE DAUGHTER. Who sends them to the madhouse?

THE LAWYER. Their own despair when they grasp the hopelessness of their efforts.

THE DAUGHTER. Has the thought not occurred to anybody, that for secret reasons it must be as it is?

THE LAWYER. Yes, those who are well off always think so.

THE DAUGHTER. That it is all right as it is?

FIRST HEAVER. And yet we are the foundations of society. If the coal is not unloaded, then there will be no fire in the kitchen stove, in the parlour grate, or in the factory furnace; then the light will go out in streets and shops and homes; then darkness and cold will descend upon you—and, therefore, we have to sweat as in hell so that the black coals may be had— And what do you do for us in return?

THE LAWYER. [*To* THE DAUGHTER] Help them!—[*Pause*] That conditions cannot be quite the same for everybody, I understand, but why should they differ so widely?

A GENTLEMAN *and* A LADY *pass across the stage.*

THE LADY. Will you come and play a game with us?

THE GENTLEMAN. No, I must take a walk, so I can eat something for dinner.

FIRST HEAVER. So that he *can* eat something?

SECOND HEAVER. So that he *can*——?

Children enter and cry with horror when they catch sight of the grimy workers.

FIRST HEAVER. They cry when they see us. They cry——

SECOND HEAVER. Damn it all!— I guess we'll have to pull out the scaffolds soon and begin to operate on this rotten body——

FIRST HEAVER. Damn it, I say, too!   [*Spits.*

THE LAWYER. [*To* THE DAUGHTER] Yes, it is all wrong. And men are not so very bad—but——

THE DAUGHTER. But——?

THE LAWYER. But the government——

THE DAUGHTER. [*Goes out, hiding her face in her hands*] This is not paradise.

COALHEAVERS. No, hell, that's what it is!

Curtain.

Fingal's Cave. Long green waves are rolling slowly into the cave. In the foreground, a siren buoy is swaying to and fro in time with the waves, but without sounding except at the indicated moment. Music of the winds. Music of the waves.

THE DAUGHTER *and* THE POET.

THE POET. Where are you leading me?

THE DAUGHTER. Far away from the noise and lament of the man-children, to the utmost end of the ocean, to the cave that we name Indra's Ear because it is the place where the king of the heavens is said to listen to the complaints of the mortals.

THE POET. What? In this place?

THE DAUGHTER. Do you see how this cave is built like a shell? Yes, you can see it. Do you know that your ear, too, is built in the form of a shell? You know it, but have not thought of it. [*She picks up a shell from the beach*] Have you not as a child held such a shell to your ear and listened—and heard the ripple of your heart-blood, the humming of your thoughts in the brain, the snapping of a thousand little worn-out threads in the tissues of your body? All that you hear in this small shell. Imagine then what may be heard in this larger one!

THE POET. [*Listening*] I hear nothing but the whispering of the wind.

THE DAUGHTER. Then I shall interpret it for you. Listen. The wail of the winds. [*Recites to subdued music:*

Born beneath the clouds of heaven,
Driven we were by the lightnings of Indra

82

Down to the sand-covered earth.
Straw from the harvested fields soiled our feet;
Dust from the high-roads,
Smoke from the cities,
Foul-smelling breaths,
Fumes from cellars and kitchens,
All we endured.
Then to the open sea we fled,
Filling our lungs with air,
Shaking our wings,
And laving our feet.

Indra, Lord of the Heavens,
Hear us!
Hear our sighing!
Unclean is the earth;
Evil is life;
Neither good nor bad
Can men be deemed.
As they can, they live,
One day at a time.
Sons of dust, through dust they journey;
Born out of dust, to dust they return.
Given they were, for trudging,
Feet, not wings for flying.
Dusty they grow—
Lies the fault then with them,
Or with Thee?

THE POET. Thus I heard it once——
THE DAUGHTER. Hush! The winds are still singing.

[*Recites to subdued music:*

We, winds that wander,
We, the air's offspring,
Bear with us men's lament.

Heard us you have
During gloom-filled Fall nights,
In chimneys and pipes,
In key-holes and door cracks,
When the rain wept on the roof:
Heard us you have
In the snowclad pine woods
Midst wintry gloom:
Heard us you have,
Crooning and moaning
In ropes and rigging
On the high-heaving sea.

It was we, the winds,
Offspring of the air,
Who learned how to grieve
Within human breasts
Through which we passed—
In sick-rooms, on battle-fields,
But mostly where the newborn
Whimpered and wailed
At the pain of living.

We, we, the winds,
We are whining and whistling:
Woe! Woe! Woe!

The Poet. It seems to me that I have already——
The Daughter. Hush! Now the waves are singing.
                              [*Recites to subdued music:*

We, we waves,
That are rocking the winds
To rest—
Green cradles, we waves!

Wet are we, and salty;
Leap like flames of fire—
Wet flames are we:
Burning, extinguishing;
Cleansing, replenishing;
Bearing, engendering.

We, we waves,
That are rocking the winds
To rest!

THE DAUGHTER. False waves and faithless! Everything on earth that is not burned, is drowned—by the waves. Look at this. [*Pointing to pile of débris*] See what the sea has taken and spoiled! Nothing but the figure-heads remain of the sunken ships—and the names: *Justice*, *Friendship*, *Golden Peace*, *Hope*—this is all that is left of *Hope*—of fickle *Hope*—Railings, tholes, bails! And lo: the life buoy—which saved itself and let distressed men perish.

THE POET. [*Searching in the pile*] Here is the name-board of the ship *Justice*. That was the one which left Fairhaven with the Blind Man's son on board. It is lost then! And with it are gone the lover of Alice, the hopeless love of Edith.

THE DAUGHTER. The Blind Man? Fairhaven? I must have been dreaming of them. And the lover of Alice, "Plain" Edith, Foulstrand and the Quarantine, sulphur and carbolic acid, the graduation in the church, the Lawyer's office, the passageway and Victoria, the Growing Castle and the Officer— All this I have been dreaming——

THE POET. It was in one of my poems.

THE DAUGHTER. You know then what poetry is——

THE POET. I know then what dreaming is— But what is poetry?

THE DAUGHTER. Not reality, but more than reality—not dreaming, but daylight dreams——

THE POET. And the man-children think that we poets are only playing—that we invent and make believe.

THE DAUGHTER. And fortunate it is, my friend, for otherwise the world would lie fallow for lack of ministration. Everybody would be stretched on his back, staring into the sky. Nobody would be touching plough or spade, hammer or plane.

THE POET. And you say this, Indra's daughter, you who belong in part up there——

THE DAUGHTER. You do right in reproaching me. Too long have I stayed down here taking mud baths like you— My thoughts have lost their power of flight; there is clay on their wings—mire on their feet—and I myself—[*raising her arms*] I sink, I sink— Help me, father, Lord of the Heavens! [*Silence*] I can no longer hear his answer. The ether no longer carries the sound from his lips to my ear's shell—the silvery thread has snapped— Woe is me, I am earthbound!

THE POET. Do you mean to ascend—soon?

THE DAUGHTER. As soon as I have consigned this mortal shape to the flames—for even the waters of the ocean cannot cleanse me. Why do you question me thus?

THE POET. Because I have a prayer——

THE DAUGHTER. What kind of prayer?

THE POET. A written supplication from humanity to the ruler of the universe, formulated by a dreamer.

THE DAUGHTER. To be presented by whom?

THE POET. By Indra's daughter.

THE DAUGHTER. Can you repeat what you have written?
THE POET. I can.
THE DAUGHTER. Speak it then.
THE POET. Better that you do it.
THE DAUGHTER. Where can I read it?
THE POET. In my mind—or here.

[*Hands her a roll of paper.*

THE DAUGHTER. [*Receives the roll, but reads without look-ing at it*] Well, by me it shall be spoken then:

"Why must you be born in anguish?
Why, O man-child, must you always
Wring your mother's heart with torture
When you bring her joy maternal,
Highest happiness yet known?
Why to life must you awaken,
Why to light give natal greeting,
With a cry of anger and of pain?
Why not meet it smiling, man-child,
When the gift of life is counted
In itself a boon unmatched?
Why like beasts should we be coming,
We of race divine and human?
Better garment craves the spirit
Than one made of filth and blood!
Need a god his teeth be changing——"

—Silence, rash one! Is it seemly
For the work to blame its maker?
No one yet has solved life's riddle.

"Thus begins the human journey
O'er a road of thorns and thistles;

If a beaten path be offered,
It is named at once forbidden;
If a flower you covet, straightway
You are told it is another's;
If a field should bar your progress,
And you dare to break across it,
You destroy your neighbour's harvest;
Others then your own will trample,
That the measure may be evened!
Every moment of enjoyment
Brings to some one else a sorrow,
But your sorrow gladdens no one,
For from sorrow naught but sorrow springs.

"Thus you journey till you die,
And your death brings others' bread."

—Is it thus that you approach,
Son of Dust, the One Most High?

THE POET.

Could the son of dust discover
Words so pure and bright and simple
That to heaven they might ascend——?

Child of gods, wilt thou interpret
Mankind's grievance in some language
That immortals understand?

THE DAUGHTER. I will.
THE POET. [*Pointing to the buoy*] What is that floating
there?— A buoy?
THE DAUGHTER. Yes.

THE POET. It looks like a lung with a windpipe.

THE DAUGHTER. It is the watchman of the seas. When danger is abroad, it sings.

THE POET. It seems to me as if the sea were rising and the waves growing larger——

THE DAUGHTER. Not unlikely.

THE POET. Woe! What do I see? A ship bearing down upon the reef.

THE DAUGHTER. What ship can that be?

THE POET. The ghost ship of the seas, I think.

THE DAUGHTER. What ship is that?

THE POET. The *Flying Dutchman*.

THE DAUGHTER. Oh, that one. Why is he punished so hard, and why does he not seek harbour?

THE POET. Because he had seven faithless wives.

THE DAUGHTER. And for this he should be punished?

THE POET. Yes, all the right-minded condemned him——

THE DAUGHTER. Strange world, this!— How can he then be freed from his curse?

THE POET. Freed?— Oh, they take good care that none is set free.

THE DAUGHTER. Why?

THE POET. Because— No, it is not the *Dutchman!* It is an ordinary ship in distress. Why does not the buoy cry out now? Look, how the sea is rising—how high the waves are—soon we shall be unable to get out of the cave! Now the ship's bell is ringing— Soon we shall have another figure-head. Cry out, buoy! Do your duty, watchman! [*The buoy sounds a four-voice chord of fifths and sixths, reminding one of fog horns*] The crew is signalling to us—but we are doomed ourselves.

THE DAUGHTER. Do you not wish to be set free?

THE POET. Yes, of course—of course, I wish it—but not just now, and not by water.

THE CREW. [*Sings in quartet*] Christ Kyrie!

THE POET. Now they are crying aloud, and so is the sea. but no one gives ear.

THE CREW. [*As before*] Christ Kyrie!

THE DAUGHTER. Who is coming there?

THE POET. Walking on the waters? There is only one who does that—and it is not Peter, the Rock, for he sank like a stone——

>   *A white light is seen shining over the water at some distance.*

THE CREW. Christ Kyrie!

THE DAUGHTER. Can this be He?

THE POET. It is He, the crucified——

THE DAUGHTER. Why—tell me—why was He crucified?

THE POET. Because He wanted to set free——

THE DAUGHTER. Who was it—I have forgotten—that crucified Him?

THE POET. All the right-minded.

THE DAUGHTER. What a strange world!

THE POET. The sea is rising. Darkness is closing in upon us. The storm is growing——

>   [THE CREW *set up a wild outcry.*

THE POET. The crew scream with horror at the sight of

their Saviour—and now—they are leaping overboard for fear of the Redeemer——

[THE CREW *utter another cry.*

THE POET. Now they are crying because they must die. Crying when they are born, and crying when they pass away!

[*The rising waves threaten to engulf the two in the cave.*

THE DAUGHTER. If I could only be sure that it is a ship——

THE POET. Really—I don't think it is a ship— It is a two-storied house with trees in front of it—and—a telephone tower—a tower that reaches up into the skies— It is the modern Tower of Babel sending wires to the upper regions—to communicate with those above——

THE DAUGHTER. Child, the human thought needs no wires to make a way for itself—the prayers of the pious penetrate the universe. It cannot be a Tower of Babel, for if you want to assail the heavens, you must do so with prayer.

THE POET. No, it is no house—no telephone tower—don't you see?

THE DAUGHTER. What are you seeing?

THE POET. I see an open space covered with snow—a drill ground— The winter sun is shining from behind a church on a hill, and the tower is casting its long shadow on the snow—Now a troop of soldiers come marching across the grounds. They march up along the tower, up the spire. Now they have reached the cross, but I have a feeling that the first one who steps on the gilded weathercock at the top must die. Now they are near it—a corporal is leading them—ha-ha! There comes a cloud sweeping across the open space, and right in front of the sun, of course—now everything is gone—the water in the cloud put out the sun's fire!— The light of the sun created the shadow picture of the tower, but the shadow picture of the cloud swallowed the shadow picture of the tower——

While THE POET *is still speaking, the stage is changed and shows once more the passageway outside the opera-house.*

THE DAUGHTER. [*To* THE PORTRESS] Has the Lord Chancellor arrived yet?

THE PORTRESS. No.

THE DAUGHTER. And the Deans of the Faculties?

THE PORTRESS. No.

THE DAUGHTER. Call them at once, then, for the door is to be opened——

THE PORTRESS. Is it so very pressing?

THE DAUGHTER. Yes, it is. For there is a suspicion that the solution of the world-riddle may be hidden behind it. Call the Lord Chancellor, and the Deans of the Four Faculties also.

[THE PORTRESS *blows in a whistle.*

THE DAUGHTER. And do not forget the Glazier and his diamond, for without them nothing can be done.

STAGE PEOPLE *enter from the left as in the earlier scene.*

THE OFFICER. [*Enters from the background, in Prince Albert and high hat, with a bunch of roses in his hand, looking radiantly happy*] Victoria!

THE PORTRESS. The young lady will be coming in a moment.

THE OFFICER. Good! The carriage is waiting, the table is set, the wine is on ice—— Permit me to embrace you, madam! [*Embraces* THE PORTRESS] Victoria!

A WOMAN'S VOICE FROM ABOVE. [*Sings*] I am here!

THE OFFICER. [*Begins to walk to and fro*] Good! I am waiting.

THE POET. It seems to me that all this has happened before——

THE DAUGHTER. So it seems to me also.

THE POET. Perhaps I have dreamt it.

THE DAUGHTER. Or put it in a poem, perhaps.

THE POET. Or put it in a poem.

THE DAUGHTER. Then you know what poetry is.

THE POET. Then I know what dreaming is.

THE DAUGHTER. It seems to me that we have said all this to each other before, in some other place.

THE POET. Then you may soon figure out what reality is.

THE DAUGHTER. Or dreaming!

THE POET. Or poetry!

> *Enter the* LORD CHANCELLOR *and the* DEANS *of the* THEOLOGICAL, PHILOSOPHICAL, MEDICAL, *and* LEGAL FACULTIES.

LORD CHANCELLOR. It is about the opening of that door, of course— What does the Dean of the Theological Faculty think of it?

DEAN OF THEOLOGY. I do not think—I believe—*Credo*——

DEAN OF PHILOSOPHY. I hold——

DEAN OF MEDICINE. I know——

DEAN OF JURISPRUDENCE. I doubt until I have evidence and witnesses.

LORD CHANCELLOR. Now they are fighting again!— Well, what does Theology believe?

THEOLOGY. I believe that this door must not be opened, because it hides dangerous truths——

PHILOSOPHY. Truth is never dangerous.

MEDICINE. What is truth?

JURISPRUDENCE. What can be proved by two witnesses.

THEOLOGY. Anything can be proved by two false witnesses —thinks the pettifogger.

PHILOSOPHY. Truth is wisdom, and wisdom, knowledge, is philosophy itself— Philosophy is the science of sciences, the knowledge of knowing, and all other sciences are its servants.

MEDICINE. Natural science is the only true science—and philosophy is no science at all. It is nothing but empty speculation.

THEOLOGY. Good!

PHILOSOPHY. [*To* THEOLOGY] Good, you say! And what are you, then? You are the arch-enemy of all knowledge; you are the very antithesis of knowledge; you are ignorance and obscuration——

MEDICINE. Good!

THEOLOGY. [*To* MEDICINE] You cry "good," you, who cannot see beyond the length of your own nose in the magnifying glass; who believes in nothing but your own unreliable senses—in your vision, for instance, which may be far-sighted, near-sighted, blind, purblind, cross-eyed, one-eyed, colour-blind, red-blind, green-blind——

MEDICINE. Idiot!

THEOLOGY. Ass!   [*They fight.*

LORD CHANCELLOR. Peace! One crow does not peck out the other's eye.

PHILOSOPHY. If I had to choose between those two, Theology and Medicine, I should choose—neither!

JURISPRUDENCE. And if I had to sit in judgment on the three of you, I should find—all guilty! You cannot agree on a single point, and you never could. Let us get back to the case in court. What is the opinion of the Lord Chancellor as to this door and its opening?

LORD CHANCELLOR. Opinion? I have no opinion whatever. I am merely appointed by the government to see that you don't break each other's arms and legs in the Council—while you are educating the young! Opinion? Why, I take mighty good care to avoid everything of the kind. Once I had one or two, but they were refuted at once. Opinions are always refuted—by their opponents, of course— But perhaps we might open the door now, even with the risk of finding some dangerous truths behind it?

JURISPRUDENCE. What is truth? What is truth?

THEOLOGY. I am the truth and the life——

PHILOSOPHY. I am the science of sciences——

MEDICINE. I am the only exact science——

JURISPRUDENCE. I doubt——   [*They fight.*

THE DAUGHTER. Instructors of the young, take shame!

JURISPRUDENCE. Lord Chancellor, as representative of the government, as head of the corps of instructors, you must prosecute this woman's offence. She has told all of you to take shame, which is an insult; and she has—in a sneering, ironical sense—called you instructors of the young, which is a slanderous speech.

THE DAUGHTER. Poor youth!

JURISPRUDENCE. She pities the young, which is to accuse us. Lord Chancellor, you must prosecute the offence.

THE DAUGHTER. Yes, I accuse you—you in a body—of sowing doubt and discord in the minds of the young.

JURISPRUDENCE. Listen to her—she herself is making the young question our authority, and then she charges us with sowing doubt. Is it not a criminal act, I ask all the right-minded?

ALL RIGHT-MINDED. Yes, it is criminal.

JURISPRUDENCE. All the right-minded have condemned you. Leave in peace with your lucre, or else——

THE DAUGHTER. My lucre? Or else? What else?

JURISPRUDENCE. Else you will be stoned.

THE POET. Or crucified.

THE DAUGHTER. I leave. Follow me, and you shall learn the riddle.

THE POET. Which riddle?

THE DAUGHTER. What did he mean with "my lucre"?

THE POET. Probably nothing at all. That kind of thing we call talk. He was just talking.

THE DAUGHTER. But it was what hurt me more than anything else!

THE POET. That is why he said it, I suppose— Men are that way.

ALL RIGHT-MINDED. Hooray! The door is open.

LORD CHANCELLOR. What was behind the door?

THE GLAZIER. I can see nothing.

LORD CHANCELLOR. He cannot see anything—of course, he cannot! Deans of the Faculties: what was behind that door?

THEOLOGY. Nothing! That is the solution of the world-riddle. In the beginning God created heaven and the earth out of nothing——

PHILOSOPHY. Out of nothing comes nothing.

MEDICINE. Yes, bosh—which is nothing!

JURISPRUDENCE. I doubt. And this is a case of deception. I appeal to all the right-minded.

THE DAUGHTER. [To THE POET] Who are the right-minded?

THE POET. Who can tell? Frequently all the right-minded consist of a single person. To-day it is me and mine; to-morrow it is you and yours. To that position you are appointed— or rather, you appoint yourself to it.

ALL RIGHT-MINDED. We have been deceived.

LORD CHANCELLOR. Who has deceived you?

ALL RIGHT-MINDED. The Daughter!

LORD CHANCELLOR. Will the Daughter please tell us what she meant by having this door opened?

THE DAUGHTER. No, friends. If I did, you would not believe me.

MEDICINE. Why, then, there is nothing there.

THE DAUGHTER. You have said it—but you have not understood.

MEDICINE. It is bosh, what she says!

ALL. Bosh!

THE DAUGHTER. [To THE POET] They are to be pitied.

THE POET. Are you in earnest?

THE DAUGHTER. Always in earnest.

THE POET. Do you think the right-minded are to be pitied also?

THE DAUGHTER. They most of all, perhaps.

THE POET. And the four faculties, too?

THE DAUGHTER. They also, and not the least. Four heads, four minds, and one body. Who made that monster?

ALL. She has not answered!

LORD CHANCELLOR. Stone her then!

THE DAUGHTER. I have answered.

LORD CHANCELLOR. Hear—she answers.

ALL. Stone her! She answers!

THE DAUGHTER. Whether she answer or do not answer, stone her! Come, prophet, and I shall tell you the riddle —but far away from here—out in the desert, where no one can hear us, no one see us, for——

THE LAWYER. [Enters and takes THE DAUGHTER by the arm] Have you forgotten your duties?

THE DAUGHTER. Oh, heavens, no! But I have higher duties.

THE LAWYER. And your child?

THE DAUGHTER. My child—what of it?

THE LAWYER. Your child is crying for you.

THE DAUGHTER. My child! Woe, I am earth-bound! And this pain in my breast, this anguish—what is it?

THE LAWYER. Don't you know?

THE DAUGHTER. No.

THE LAWYER. It is remorse.

THE DAUGHTER. Is that remorse?

THE LAWYER. Yes, and it follows every neglected duty; every pleasure, even the most innocent, if innocent pleasures exist, which seems doubtful; and every suffering inflicted upon one's fellow-beings.

THE DAUGHTER. And there is no remedy?

THE LAWYER. Yes, but only one. It consists in doing your duty at once——

THE DAUGHTER. You look like a demon when you speak that word duty— And when, as in my case, there are two duties to be met?

THE LAWYER. Meet one first, and then the other.

THE DAUGHTER. The highest first—therefore, you look after my child, and I shall do my duty——

THE LAWYER. Your child suffers because it misses you— can you bear to know that a human being is suffering for your sake?

THE DAUGHTER. Now strife has entered my soul—it is rent in two, and the halves are being pulled in opposite directions!

THE LAWYER. Such, you know, are life's little discords.

THE DAUGHTER. Oh, how it is pulling!

THE POET. If you could only know how I have spread sorrow and ruin around me by the exercise of my calling— and note that I say *calling*, which carries with it the highest duty of all—then you would not even touch my hand.

THE DAUGHTER. What do you mean?

THE POET. I had a father who put his whole hope on me as his only son, destined to continue his enterprise. I ran away from the business college. My father grieved himself to death. My mother wanted me to be religious, and I could not do what she wanted—and she disowned me. I had a friend who assisted me through trying days of need—and that friend acted as a tyrant against those on whose behalf I was speaking and writing. And I had to strike down my friend and benefactor in order to save my soul. Since then I have had no peace. Men call me devoid of honour, infamous—and it does not help that my conscience says, "you have done right," for in the next moment it is saying, "you have done wrong." Such is life.

THE DAUGHTER. Come with me into the desert.

THE LAWYER. Your child!

THE DAUGHTER. [*Indicating all those present*] Here are my children. By themselves they are good, but if they only come together, then they quarrel and turn into demons—Farewell!

Outside the castle. The same scenery as in the first scene of the first act. But now the ground in front of the castle wall is covered with flowers—blue monk's-hood or aconite. On the roof of the castle, at the very top of its lantern, there is a chrysanthemum bud ready to open. The castle windows are illuminated with candles.

THE DAUGHTER *and* THE POET.

THE DAUGHTER. The hour is not distant when, with the help of the flames, I shall once more ascend to the ether. It is what you call to die, and what you approach in fear.

THE POET. Fear of the unknown.

THE DAUGHTER. Which is known to you.

THE POET. Who knows it?

THE DAUGHTER. All! Why do you not believe your prophets?

THE POET. Prophets have always been disbelieved. Why is that so? And "if God has spoken, why will men not believe then?" His convincing power ought to be irresistible

THE DAUGHTER. Have you always doubted?

THE POET. No. I have had certainty many times. But after a while it passed away, like a dream when you wake up.

THE DAUGHTER. It is not easy to be human!

THE POET. You see and admit it?

THE DAUGHTER. I do.

THE POET. Listen! Was it not Indra that once sent his son down here to receive the complaints of mankind?

THE DAUGHTER. Thus it happened—and how was he received?

THE POET. How did he fill his mission?—to answer with another question.

THE DAUGHTER. And if I may reply with still another—was not man's position bettered by his visit to the earth? Answer truly!

THE POET. Bettered?— Yes, a little. A very little— But instead of asking questions—will you not tell the riddle?

THE DAUGHTER. Yes. But to what use? You will not believe me.

THE POET. In you I shall believe, for I know who you are.

THE DAUGHTER. Then I shall tell! In the morning of the ages, before the sun was shining, Brahma, the divine primal force, let himself be persuaded by Maya, the world-mother, to propagate himself. This meeting of the divine primal matter with the earth-matter was the fall of heaven into sin. Thus the world, existence, mankind, are nothing but a phantom, an appearance, a dream-image——

THE POET. My dream!

THE DAUGHTER. A dream of truth! But in order to free themselves from the earth-matter, the offspring of Brahma seek privation and suffering. There you have suffering as a liberator. But this craving for suffering comes into conflict with the craving for enjoyment, or love—do you now understand what love is, with its utmost joys merged into its utmost sufferings, with its mixture of what is most sweet and most bitter? Can you now grasp what woman is? Woman, through whom sin and death found their way into life?

THE POET. I understand!— And the end?

THE DAUGHTER. You know it: conflict between the pain of enjoyment and the pleasure of suffering—between the pangs of the penitent and the joys of the prodigal——

THE POET. A conflict it is then?

THE DAUGHTER. Conflict between opposites produces energy, as fire and water give the power of steam——

THE POET. But peace? Rest?

THE DAUGHTER. Hush! You must ask no more, and I can no longer answer. The altar is already adorned for the sacrifice—the flowers are standing guard—the candles are lit—there are white sheets in the windows—spruce boughs have been spread in the gateway——

THE POET. And you say this as calmly as if for you suffering did not exist!

THE DAUGHTER. You think so?— I have suffered all your sufferings, but in a hundredfold degree, for my sensations were so much more acute——

THE POET. Relate your sorrow!

THE DAUGHTER. Poet, could you tell yours so that not one word went too far? Could your word at any time approach your thought?

THE POET. No, you are right! To myself I appeared like one struck dumb, and when the mass listened admiringly to my song, I found it mere noise—for this reason, you see, I have always felt ashamed when they praised me.

THE DAUGHTER. And then you ask me— Look me straight in the eye!

THE POET. I cannot bear your glance——

THE DAUGHTER. How could you bear my word then, were I to speak in your tongue?

THE POET. But tell me at least before you go: from what did you suffer most of all down here?

THE DAUGHTER. From—*being:* to feel my vision weakened by an eye, my hearing blunted by an ear, and my thought, my bright and buoyant thought, bound in labyrinthine coils of fat. You have seen a brain—what roundabout and sneaking paths——

THE POET. Well, that is because all the right-minded think crookedly!

THE DAUGHTER. Malicious, always malicious, all of you!

THE POET. How could one possibly be otherwise?

THE DAUGHTER. First of all I now shake the dust from my feet—the dirt and the clay—

[*Takes off her shoes and puts them into the fire.*

THE PORTRESS. [*Puts her shawl into the fire*] Perhaps I may burn my shawl at the same time?   [*Goes out.*

THE OFFICER. [*Enters*] And I my roses, of which only the thorns are left.   [*Goes out.*

THE BILLPOSTER. [*Enters*] My bills may go, but never the dipnet!   [*Goes out.*

THE GLAZIER. [*Enters*] The diamond that opened the door—good-bye!   [*Goes out.*

THE LAWYER. [*Enters*] The minutes of the great process concerning the pope's beard or the water loss in the sources of the Ganges.   [*Goes out.*

MASTER OF QUARANTINE. [*Enters*] A small contribution in shape of the black mask that made me a blackamoor against my will!   [*Goes out.*

VICTORIA. [*Enters*] My beauty, my sorrow!   [*Goes out.*

EDITH. [*Enters*] My plainness, my sorrow!   [*Goes out.*

THE BLINDMAN. [*Enters; puts his hand into the fire*] I give
my hand for my eye.   [*Goes out.*

DON JUAN *in his wheel chair;* SHE *and* THE FRIEND.

DON JUAN. Hurry up! Hurry up! Life is short!
                                   [*Leaves with the other two.*

THE POET. I have read that when the end of life draws
near, everything and everybody rushes by in continuous re-
view— Is this the end?

THE DAUGHTER. Yes, it is my end. Farewell!

THE POET. Give us a parting word.

THE DAUGHTER. No, I cannot. Do you believe that your
words can express our thoughts?

DEAN OF THEOLOGY. [*Enters in a rage*] I am cast off by
God and persecuted by man; I am deserted by the government and scorned by my colleagues! How am I to believe
when nobody else believes? How am I to defend a god that
does not defend his own? Bosh, that's what it is!
                          [*Throws a book on the fire and goes out.*

THE POET. [*Snatches the book out of the fire*] Do you know
what it is? A martyrology, a calendar with a martyr for
each day of the year.

THE DAUGHTER. Martyr?

THE POET. Yes, one that has been tortured and killed on
account of his faith! Tell me why?— Do you think that all
who are tortured suffer, and that all who are killed feel pain?
Suffering is said to be salvation, and death a liberation.

CHRISTINE. [*With slips of paper*] I paste, I paste until
there is nothing more to paste——

THE POET. And if heaven should split in twain, you would
try to paste it together— Away!

CHRISTINE. Are there no double windows in this castle?

THE POET. Not one, I tell you.

CHRISTINE. Well, then I'll go.   [*Goes out.*

THE DAUGHTER.

The parting hour has come, the end draws near.
And now farewell, thou dreaming child of man,
Thou singer, who alone knows how to live!
When from thy winged flight above the earth
At times thou sweepest downward to the dust,
It is to touch it only, not to stay!

And as I go—how, in the parting hour,
As one must leave for e'er a friend, a place,
The heart with longing swells for what one loves,
And with regret for all wherein one failed!
O, now the pangs of life in all their force
I feel· I know at last the lot of man——
Regretfully one views what once was scorned;
For sins one never sinned remorse is felt;
To stay one craves, but equally to leave:
As if to horses tied that pull apart,
One's heart is split in twain, one's feelings rent,
By indecision, contrast, and discord.

Farewell! To all thy fellow-men make known
That where I go I shall forget them not;
And in thy name their grievance shall be placed
Before the throne.   Farewell!

> *She goes into the castle. Music is heard. The background is lit up by the burning castle and reveals a wall of human faces, questioning, grieving, despairing. As the castle breaks into flames, the bud on the roof opens into a gigantic chrysanthemum flower.*

Curtain.

THE LINK
A TRAGEDY IN ONE ACT

1877

CHARACTERS

THE JUDGE, 27 *years*
THE PASTOR, 60 *years*
THE BARON, 42 *years*
THE BARONESS, 40 *years*
ALEXANDER EKLUND
EMMANUEL WICKBERG
CARL JOHAN SJÖBERG
ERIC OTTO BOMAN
ÄRENFRID SÖDERBERG
OLOF ANDERSSON OF WIK
CARL PETER ANDERSSON OF
    BERGA
ALEX WALLIN
ANDERS ERIC RUTH
SWEN OSCAR ERLIN
AUGUST ALEXANDER VASS
LUDWIG ÖSTMAN

Jurors

THE CLERK OF THE COURT
THE SHERIFF
THE CONSTABLE
THE LAWYER
ALEXANDERSSON. *a farmer*
ALMA JONSSON, *a servant girl*
THE MILKMAID
THE FARM HAND
SPECTATORS

THE LINK

A court-room.   Door and windows in the background.   Through the windows are seen the churchyard and the bell-tower. Door on the right.   On the left, the desk of the judge on a platform.   The front side of the desk is decorated in gold, with the judicial emblems of the sword and the scales.   On both sides of the desk are placed chairs and small tables for the twelve jurors.   In the centre of the room, benches for the spectators.   Along the sides of the room are cupboards built into the walls.   On the doors of these are posted court notices and schedules of market tolls.

SCENE I

THE SHERIFF *and* THE CONSTABLE

THE SHERIFF. Did you ever see such a lot of people at the summer sessions before?

THE CONSTABLE. Not in fifteen years, or since we had the big murder at Alder Lake.

SHERIFF. Well, this story here is almost as good as a double parricide.   That the Baron and the Baroness are going to separate is scandal enough, but when on top of it the families take to wrangling about properties and estates, then it's easy to see that there's going to be a hot time.   The only thing wanting now is that they get to fighting over the child, too, and then King Solomon himself can't tell what's right.

CONSTABLE. What is there behind this case anyhow?   Some say this and some say that, but the blame ought to rest on somebody?

107

SHERIFF. I don't know about that. Sometimes it is nobody's fault when two quarrel, and then again one alone is to
blame for the quarrel of two. Now take my old shrew, for
instance, she's running around at home scolding for dear life
all by herself when I am away, they tell me. Besides, this
is not just a quarrel, but a full-fledged criminal case, and in
most such one party is complainant, or the one that has been
wronged, and the other is defendant, or the one that has committed the crime. But in this case it is not easy to tell who is
guilty, for both parties are at once complainants and defen-
dants.

CONSTABLE. Well, well, queer things do happen these days.
It's as if the women had gone crazy. My old one has spells
when she says that I should bear children also, if there was any
justice in things—just as if the Lord didn't know how he made
his own creatures. And then I get long rigmaroles about her
being human also, just as if I didn't know that before, or had
said anything to the contrary; and of her being tired of acting
as my servant girl, when, for a fact, I am not much better than
her hired man.

SHERIFF. So-o. So you have got that kind of plague in
your house too. Mine reads a paper she gets at the manor, and
then she tells me as something wonderful, one day, that some
farmer's lass has turned mason, and the next that an old
woman has set upon and beaten her sick husband. I cannot
quite get at what's the meaning of it all, but it looks most as
if she was mad at me for being a man.

CONSTABLE. Mighty queer, that's what it is. [*Offers snuff*]
Fine weather we're having. The rye is standing as thick as
the hairs in a fox fell, and we got over the black frosts without
a hitch.

SHERIFF. There is nothing of mine growing, and good
years are bad for me: no executions and no auctions. Do

you know anything about the new judge who is going to hold court to-day?

CONSTABLE. Not much, but I understand he's a youngster who has just got his appointment and is going to sit for the first time now——

SHERIFF. And they say he is religious. Hm!

CONSTABLE. Hm-hm!— They're taking an awful time over the church services this year.

SHERIFF. [*Puts a big Bible on the judge's desk and a smaller one on each one of the jurors' tables*] It cannot be long till they're done now, for they have been at it most of an hour.

CONSTABLE. He's a wonder at preaching, is the Pastor, once he gets going. [*Pause*] Are the parties to put in a personal appearance?

SHERIFF. Both of them, so I guess we'll have some scrapping— [*The bell in the tower begins to ring*] There, now they're done— Just give the tables a wiping, and I think we are ready to start.

CONSTABLE. And there's ink in all the wells?

SCENE II

The BARON *and the* BARONESS *enter.*

BARON. [*In a low voice to the* BARONESS] Then, before we part for a year, we are perfectly agreed on all points. First, no recriminations in court?

BARONESS. Do you think I would care to lay open the intimate details of our common life before a lot of curious peasants?

BARON. So much the better! And further: you keep the child during the year of separation, provided it may visit me when I so desire, and provided it is educated in accordance with the principles laid down by me and approved by you?

BARONESS. Exactly!

BARON. And out of the income from the estate I give you three thousand crowns during the year of separation?

BARONESS. Agreed.

BARON. Then I have nothing more to add, but ask only to bid you good-bye. Why we part is known only to you and me, and for the sake of our son no one else must know it. But for his sake I beg you also: start no fight, lest we be goaded into soiling the names of his parents. It is more than likely, anyhow, that life in its cruelty will make him suffer for our divorce.

BARONESS. I don't care to fight as long as I may keep my child.

BARON. Let us then concentrate our attention on the child's welfare and forget what has happened between us. And remember another thing: if we fight about the child and question each other's fitness to take care of it, the judge may take it away from both of us and put it with some of those religious people who will bring it up in hatred and contempt for its parents.

BARONESS. That's impossible!

BARON. Such, my dear, is the law.

BARONESS. It is a stupid law.

BARON. Maybe, but it holds; and for you no less than for others.

BARONESS. It is unnatural! And I should never submit to it.

BARON. You don't have to, as we have decided to raise no objections against each other. We have never agreed before, but on this one point we are at one, are we not: to part without any kind of hostility? [*To the* SHERIFF] Could the Baroness be permitted to wait in that room over there?

SHERIFF. Certainly, walk right in.

> *The* BARON *escorts the* BARONESS *to the door on the right and leaves then himself through the door in the background.*

SCENE III

The SHERIFF.   *The* CONSTABLE.   *The* LAWYER. ALMA
JONSSON.   *The* MILKMAID.   *The* FARM HAND.

LAWYER. [*To* ALMA JONSSON] Look here, my girl: that you have stolen, I don't doubt for a moment; but as your master has no witnesses to it, you are not guilty. But as your master has called you a thief in the presence of two witnesses, he is guilty of slander. And now you are complainant and he defendant. Remember this one thing: the first duty of a criminal is—to deny!

ALMA JONSSON. But please, sir, didn't you just say I was no criminal, and master was?

LAWYER. You are a criminal because you have committed a theft, but as you have called for a lawyer, it is my unmistakable duty to clear you and convict your master. Therefore, and for the last time: deny! [*To the witnesses*] And as to the witnesses, what are they going to testify? Listen: a good witness sticks to the case. Now you must bear in mind that the question is not whether Alma has stolen anything or not, but only whether Alexandersson said that she had stolen. For, mark you, he has no right to prove his assertions, but we have. Why it should be so, the devil only knows! But that's none of your business. Therefore: keep your tongues straight and your fingers on the Bible!

MILKMAID. Lord, but I'm that scared, for I don't know what I'm going to say!

FARM HAND. You say as I do, and then you won't be lying.

SCENE IV

The JUDGE *and the* PASTOR *enter.*

JUDGE. Permit me to thank you for the sermon, Pastor.

PASTOR. Oh, don't mention it, Judge.

JUDGE. Yes—for, as you know, this is my first court. To tell the truth, I have felt some fear of this career, into which I have been thrown almost against my will. For one thing, the laws are so imperfect, the judicial practices so uncertain, and human nature so full of falsehood and dissimulation, that I have often wondered how a judge could dare to express any definite opinion at all. And to-day you have revived all my old fears.

PASTOR. To be conscientious is a duty, of course, but to be sentimental about it won't do. And as everything else on this earth is imperfect, there is no reason why we should expect judges and judgments to be perfect.

JUDGE. That may be, but it does not prevent me from harbouring a sense of tremendous responsibility, as I have men's fates in my hand, and a word spoken by me may show its effects through generations. I am especially thinking of this separation suit started by the Baron and his wife, and I have to ask you—you who have administered the two prescribed warnings before the Vestry Board—what is your view concerning their mutual relations and relative guilt?

PASTOR. In other words, Judge, you would either put me in your own place or base your decision on my testimony. And all I can do is to refer you to the minutes of the board.

JUDGE. Yes, the minutes— I know them. But it is just what does not appear in the minutes that I need to know.

PASTOR. What charges the couple made against each other at the private hearings must be my secret. And besides, how can I know who told the truth and who lied? I have to tell you what I told them: there is no reason why I should believe more in one than in the other.

JUDGE. But were you not able to form some kind of opinion in the matter during the hearings?

PASTOR. When I heard one, I formed one opinion, and another when I was hearing the other. In a word: I have no settled view in this question.

JUDGE. But I am to express a definite view— I, who know nothing at all.

PASTOR. That is the heavy task of the judge, which I could never undertake.

JUDGE. But there are witnesses to be heard? Evidence to be obtained?

PASTOR. No, they are not accusing each other in public. And furthermore: two false witnesses will furnish sufficient proof, and a perjurer will do just as well. Do you think I would base my judgment on servant gossip, on the loose-tongued chatter of envious neighbours, or on the spiteful partisanship of relatives?

JUDGE. You are a terrible sceptic, Pastor.

PASTOR. Well, one gets to be so after sixty, and particularly after having tended souls for forty years. The habit of lying clings like original sin, and I believe that all men lie. As children we lie out of fear; as grown-ups, out of interest, need, instinct for self-preservation; and I have known those who lied out of sheer kindliness. In the present case, and in so far as this married couple is concerned, I fear you will find it very hard to figure out who has told most of the truth, and all I can do is to warn you against being caught in the snares set by preconceived opinions. You were married not long ago yourself, and you are still under the spell of the young woman's witchery. For this reason you may easily become prejudiced in favor of a young and charming lady, who is an unhappy wife and a mother besides. On the other hand, you have also recently become a father, and as such you cannot escape being moved by the impending separation of the father from his child. Beware of sympathy with either side, for sympathy with one is cruelty to the other.

JUDGE. One thing will make my task more easy at least, and that is their mutual agreement on the principal points.

PASTOR. Don't rely too much on that, for it is what they all say. And when they appear in court, the smouldering fire breaks into open flames. In this case a tiny spark will be enough to start a conflagration. Here comes the jury. Well, good-by for a while! I stay, although I shall not be seen.

SCENE V

The TWELVE JURORS *enter. The* SHERIFF *rings a bell from the open doorway in the background. The members of the Court take their seats.* SPECTATORS *pour into the room.*

JUDGE. With a reminder of the provisions in Chapter Eleven, Sections Five, Six, and Eight, of the Criminal Code, as to the peace and order that must be maintained in Court, I hereby declare the proceedings of the Court opened. [*Whispers to the* CLERK OF THE COURT; *then*] Will the newly chosen jury please take the oath.

JURORS. [*Rise, each one putting the fingers of one hand on*

*the Bible in front of him; then they speak in unison except
when their names are being read out*]

> I, Alexander Eklund;
> I, Emmanuel Wickberg;
> I, Carl Johan Sjöberg;
> I, Eric Otto Boman;
> I, Ärenfrid Söderberg;
> I, Olof Andersson of Wik;
> I, Carl Peter Andersson of Berga;
> I, Axel Wallin;
> I, Anders Eric Ruth;
> I, Swen Oscar Erlin;
> I, August Alexander Vass;
> I, Ludwig Östman;

[*all at once, keeping time and speaking with low voices in a low
pitch*] promise and swear by God and His Holy Gospel, that
I will and shall, according to my best reason and conscience,
judge rightly in all cases, no less for the poor than for the
rich, and decide in accordance with the law of God and that
of this country, as well as its legal statutes: [*in a higher pitch
and with raised voices*] never tamper with the law or further
any wrong, for the sake of either kinship by blood, kinship
by marriage, friendship, envy, ill-will, or fear; nor for the
sake of bribe or gift or any other cause, under any form what-
soever: and not make him responsible who has no guilt, or
set him free who is guilty. [*Raising their voices still further*]
Neither before judgment nor afterward, neither to parties in
court nor to others, am I to discover such counsel as may be
taken by the Court behind closed doors. All this I will and
shall faithfully keep as an honest and upright judge, without
fell deceit or design— [*Pause*] So help God my life and soul!

> [*The* JURORS *sit down.*

JUDGE. [*To the* SHERIFF] Call the case of Alma Jonsson
against the farmer Alexandersson.

SCENE VI

Enter the LAWYER, ALEXANDERSSON, ALMA JONSSON, *the* MILKMAID, *the* FARM HAND.

SHERIFF. [*Calls out*] The servant girl Alma Jonsson and the farmer Alexandersson.

LAWYER. I wish to present my power of attorney for the complainant.

JUDGE. [*Examines the submitted document; then*] The servant girl Alma Jonsson has had writ served on her former master, Alexandersson, bringing charges under Chapter Sixteen, Section Eight, of the Criminal Code, providing for imprisonment of not more than six months, or a fine, because Alexandersson has called her a thief without supporting his accusation or making legal charges. What have you to say, Alexandersson?

ALEXANDERSSON. I called her a thief because I caught her stealing.

JUDGE. Have you witnesses to her theft?

ALEXANDERSSON. No, as luck would have it, there's no witnesses, for I mostly go about by myself.

JUDGE. Why did you not make a charge against her?

ALEXANDERSSON. Well, I never go to court. And then it isn't the usage among us masters to prosecute household thefts, partly because there are so many of 'em, and partly because we don't like to spoil a servant's whole future.

JUDGE. Alma Jonsson, what have you to say in answer to this?

ALMA JONSSON. Ya-es——

LAWYER. You keep quiet! Alma Jonsson, who is not a defendant in this case, but the complainant, asks to have her

witnesses heard in order that she may prove the slander ut-
tered against her by Alexandersson.

JUDGE. As Alexandersson has admitted the slander, I shall
ask for no witnesses.   On the other hand, it is of importance
for me to know whether Alma Jonsson be guilty of the offence
mentioned, for if Alexandersson had reasonable grounds for
his utterance, this will be held a mitigating circumstance when
sentence is passed.

LAWYER. I must take exception to the statement made by
the Court, for by Chapter Sixteen, Section Thirteen, of the
Criminal Code, one charged with slander is denied the right
to bring evidence as to the truth of his defamation.

JUDGE. Parties, witnesses, and spectators will retire so that
the Court may consider the case.

[*All go out except the members of the Court.*

SCENE VII

THE COURT.

JUDGE. Is Alexandersson an honest and reliable man?
ALL THE JURORS. Alexandersson is a reliable man.

JUDGE. Is Alma Jonsson known as an honest servant?

ERIC OTTO BOMAN. I had to discharge Alma Jonsson last
year for petty thievery.

JUDGE. And nevertheless I have now to fine Alexandersson.
There is no way out of it.   Is he poor?

LUDWIG ÖSTMAN. He's behind with his Crown taxes, and
his crop failed last year.   So I guess the fine will be more than
he can carry.

JUDGE. And yet I can find no reason to postpone the case,
as it is a clear one, and Alexandersson has no right to prove

anything on his side. Has any one here anything to add or object?

ALEXANDER EKLUND. I would just ask leave to make a general reflection. A case like this, where one not only innocent, but offended against, has to take the punishment, while the thief has his so-called honour restored, may easily bring about that people grow less forbearing toward their fellow-men, and that taking cases to court grows more common.

JUDGE. This is quite possible, but general reflections have no place in the proceedings, and the Court has to make a decision. Consequently my one question to the jury is: can Alexandersson be held guilty under Chapter Sixteen, Section Thirteen, of the Criminal Code?

ALL THE JURORS. Yes.

JUDGE. [*To the* SHERIFF] Call in the parties and the witnesses.

SCENE VIII

ALL *return.*

JUDGE. In the case of Alma Jonsson against the farmer Alexandersson, Alexandersson is sentenced to pay a fine of one hundred crowns for slander.

ALEXANDERSSON. But I saw her stealing with my own eyes!— That's what one gets for being kind!

LAWYER. [*To* ALMA JONSSON] What did I tell you! If you only deny, everything is all right. Alexandersson acted like a fool and denied nothing. If I had been his counsel, and he had denied the charge, I should have challenged your witnesses, and there you would have been!— Now we'll go out and settle up this business.

[*Goes out with* ALMA JONSSON *and the witnesses.*

ALEXANDERSSON. [*To the* SHERIFF] And perhaps I have now got to give Alma her papers and write down that she has been honest and faithful?

SHERIFF. That's none of my concern!

ALEXANDERSSON. [*To the* CONSTABLE] And for a thing like this I am to lose house and land! Who'd believe it, that justice means honour for the thief and a flogging for him that's robbed! Damn it!— Come and have a cup of coffee with a stick in it afterward, Öman.

CONSTABLE. I'll come, but don't make a row.

ALEXANDERSSON. Yes, I'll be damned if I don't, even if it should cost me three months!

CONSTABLE. Now please don't make a row—don't make a row!

SCENE IX

The BARON *and the* BARONESS *enter after awhile.*

JUDGE. [*To the* SHERIFF] Call the separation suit of Baron Sprengel and his wife, born Malmberg.

SHERIFF. Separation suit of Baron Sprengel and his wife, born Malmberg.

The BARON *and the* BARONESS *enter.*

JUDGE. In the proceedings entered against his wife, Baron Sprengel declares his intention of not continuing the marriage, and requests that, as the warnings of the Vestry Board have proved fruitless, order be issued for a year's separation in bed and board. What objection have you to make to this, Baroness?

BARONESS. To the separation I make no objection at all, if I can only have my child. That is my condition.

JUDGE. The law recognises no conditions in a case like this, and it is for the Court to dispose of the child.

BARONESS. Why, that's very peculiar!

JUDGE. For this reason it is of utmost importance that the Court learn who has caused the dissension leading to this suit. According to appended minutes of the Vestry Board, it appears that the wife has admitted having at times shown a quarrelsome and difficult disposition, while the husband has admitted no fault. Thus, Baroness, you appear to have admitted——

BARONESS. That's a lie!

JUDGE. I find it difficult to believe that the minutes of the Vestry Board, countersigned by the Pastor and eight other trustworthy men, can be inaccurate.

BARONESS. The report is false!

JUDGE. Such remarks cannot be made with impunity before this Court.

BARON. May I call attention to the fact that I have voluntarily surrendered the child to the Baroness on certain conditions?

JUDGE. And I have to repeat once more what I said before, namely, that the case will be decided by the Court and not by the parties to it. Therefore: you deny having caused any dissension, Baroness?

BARONESS. Indeed, I do! And it is not the fault of one that two quarrel.

JUDGE. This is no quarrel, Baroness, but a criminal case; and furthermore, you seem now to be displaying a contentious temperament as well as inconsiderate behaviour.

BARONESS. Then you don't know my husband.

JUDGE. Will you please explain yourself, for I can base no decision on mere insinuations.

BARON. Then I must ask to have the case dismissed, so that I can obtain separation in other ways.

JUDGE. The case is already before the Court and will have to be carried to its conclusion— Baroness, you maintain then that your husband has caused the estrangement. Can this be proved?

BARONESS. Yes, it can be proved.

JUDGE. Please do so then, but bear in mind that it is a question of depriving the Baron of his parental rights and also of his rights to the property.

BARONESS. He has forfeited it many times over, and not the least when he denied me sleep and food.

BARON. I feel compelled to state that I have never refused to let the Baroness sleep. I have merely asked her not to sleep in the afternoon, because thereby the house was neglected and the child left without proper care. As to food, I have always left such matters to my wife, and I have only objected to some extravagant entertainments, as the neglected household could not bear such expenses.

BARONESS. And he has let me lie sick without calling in a physician.

BARON. The Baroness would always be taken sick when she could not have her own way, but that kind of ailment did not last long as a rule. After I had brought a specialist from the city, and he had declared it to be nothing but tricks, I did not judge it necessary to call a physician the next time the Baroness was taken sick—because the new pier-glass cost fifty crowns less than originally intended.

JUDGE. All this is not of such nature that it can be considered when such a serious case has to be decided. There must be some deeper motives.

BARONESS. It ought to be counted a motive that the father will not permit the mother to bring up her own child.

BARON. First of all, the Baroness left the care of the child to a maid, and whenever she tried to assist, things went wrong. Secondly, she tried to bring up the boy as a woman, and not as a man.   For instance, she dressed him as a girl until he was four years old; and to this very day, when he is eight years old, he carries his hair long as a girl, is forced to sew and crochet, and plays with dolls; all of which I regard as injurious to the child's normal development into a man.   On the other hand, she has amused herself by dressing up the daughters of our tenants as boys, cutting their hair short, and putting them to work on things generally handled by boys.   In a word, I took charge of my son's education because I noticed symptoms of mental derangement which before this have led to offences against the Eighteenth Chapter of the Criminal Code.

JUDGE. And yet you are now willing to leave the child in the hands of the mother?

BARON. Yes, for I have never been able to contemplate such a cruelty as to separate mother and child—and also because the mother has promised to mend her ways.   And for that matter, I had only promised conditionally, and with the understanding that the law was not to be invoked in the matter. But since we have not been able to keep away from recriminations, I have changed my mind—especially as, from being the complainant, I have been turned into a defendant.

BARONESS. That's the way this man always keeps his promises.

BARON. My promises, like those of other people, have always been conditional, and I have kept them as long as the conditions were observed.

BARONESS. In the same way he had promised me personal freedom within the marriage.

BARON. Naturally with the provision that the laws of decency were kept inviolate; but when all bounds were exceeded,

and when ideas of license appeared under the name of freedom, then I regarded my promise as annulled.

BARONESS. And for this reason he tormented me with the
most absurd jealousy, and that is generally enough to make a
common life unbearable.   He even made himself ridiculous
to the extent of being jealous of the doctor.

BARON. This alleged jealousy may be reduced to an advice on my part against the employment of a notorious and
tattling masseur for an ailment commonly treated by women—
unless the Baroness is having in mind the occasion when I
showed our steward the door for smoking in my drawing-room
and offering cigars to my wife.   .

BARONESS. As we have not been able to keep away from
scandal-mongering, it is just as well that the whole truth should
get out: the Baron has been guilty of adultery.   Is not this
enough to make him unworthy of bringing up my child alone?

JUDGE. Can you prove this, Baroness?

BARONESS. Yes, I can, and here are letters that show.

JUDGE. [*Receiving the letters*] How long ago did this happen?

BARONESS. A year ago.

JUDGE. Of course, the time limit for prosecution has already expired, but the fact itself weighs heavily against the
husband and may cause him to lose the child entirely as well
as a part of the marriage portion.   Do you admit the truth
of this charge, Baron?

BARON. Yes, with remorse and mortification; but there
were circumstances which ought to be held extenuating.   I
was forced into humiliating celibacy by the calculated cold-
ness of the Baroness, although I, and in all courtesy, asked
as a favour, what the law allowed me to demand as a right.   I
tired of buying her love, she having prostituted our marriage by
selling her favours first for power and later for presents and

money; and in the end I found myself compelled, with the express consent of the Baroness, to take up an irregular relationship.

JUDGE. Had you given your consent, Baroness?

BARONESS. No, that is not true! I demand proofs!

BARON. It is true, but I cannot prove it, since the only witness, my wife, denies it.

JUDGE. What is unproved need not be untrue, but a compact of this kind, trespassing upon prevailing laws, must be held a *pactum turpe* and invalid in itself. Baron, so far everything is against you.

BARONESS. And as the Baron has confessed his guilt with remorse and shame, I, who have now become complainant instead of defendant, ask that the Court proceed to render a decision, as further details are not needed.

JUDGE. In my capacity as presiding officer of this Court, I wish to hear what the Baron has to say in justification, or at least in palliation.

BARON. I have just admitted the charge of adultery and have advanced as extenuating circumstances, partly that it was the result of pressing need when, after ten years of married life, I suddenly found myself unmarried, and partly that it was done with the consent of the Baroness herself. As I have now come to believe that all this was a trap set to make a case against me, it is my duty, for the sake of my son, to hold back no further——

BARONESS. [*Exclaims instinctively*] Axel!

BARON. What caused me to break my marital vows was the faithlessness of the Baroness.

JUDGE. Baron, can you prove that the Baroness has been faithless to you?

BARON. No! For I was concerned about the honour of the family, and I destroyed all proofs that I obtained. But I still venture to believe that, in this matter, the Baroness will stand by the confession she once made to me.

JUDGE. Baroness, do you admit this offence as preceding and, therefore, probably causing the lapse of the Baron?

BARONESS. No!

JUDGE. Are you willing to repeat under oath that you are innocent of this charge?

BARONESS. Yes!

BARON. Good heavens! No, she must not do that! No perjury for my sake!

JUDGE. I ask once more: is the Baroness willing to take the oath?

BARONESS. Yes.

BARON. Permit me to suggest that the Baroness just now appears as complainant, and a complaint is not made under oath.

JUDGE. As you have charged her with a criminal offence, she is defendant. What does the Jury hold?

EMMANUEL WICKBERG. As the Baroness is a party to this suit, it seems to me that she can hardly be allowed to testify in her own behalf.

SWEN OSCAR ERLIN. It seems to me that if the Baroness is to testify under oath, then the Baron should also be allowed to do so in the same matter, but as oath may not be put against oath, the whole matter remains in the dark.

AUGUST ALEXANDER VASS. I should say that it is not a question of testifying under oath here, but of taking an oath on one's own innocence.

ANDERS ERIC RUTH. Well, isn't that the question which has to be settled first of all?

AXEL WALLIN. But not in the presence of the parties, as the deliberations of the Court are not public.

CARL JOHAN SJÖBERG. The right of the jury to express itself is not limited or conditioned by secrecy.

JUDGE. Out of so many meanings I can get no guidance. But as the guilt of the Baron can be proved, and that of the Baroness still remains unproved, I must demand that the Baroness take oath on her innocence.

BARONESS. I am ready!

JUDGE. No, wait a moment!— Baron, if you were granted time, would you be able to produce evidence or witnesses in support of your charge?

BARON. This I neither can nor will do, as I am not anxious to see my dishonour made public.

JUDGE. The proceedings of the Court will be adjourned while I consult with the chairman of the Vestry Board.

[*Steps down and goes out to the right.*

SCENE X

The JURORS *confer in low tones among themselves. The* BARON *and the* BARONESS *in the background. The* SPECTATORS *form groups and talk.*

BARON. [*To the* BARONESS] You do not shrink from perjuring yourself?

BARONESS. I shrink from nothing when my child is concerned.

BARON. But if I have proofs?

BARONESS. Well, you have not.

BARON. The letters were burned, but certified copies of them are still in existence.

BARONESS. You lie to frighten me!

BARON. To show you how deeply I love my child, and to save the mother at least, as I seem to be lost, you—may have the proofs. But don't be ungrateful.

[*Hands her a bundle of letters.*

BARONESS. That you are a liar, I knew before, but that you were scoundrel enough to have the letters copied, that I could never have believed.

BARON. That is your thanks! But now both of us are lost.

BARONESS. Yes, let both go down—then there will be an end to the fight——

BARON. Is it better for the child to lose both its parents and be left alone in the world?

BARONESS. That will never occur!

BARON. Your absurd conceit, which makes you think yourself above all laws and above other human beings, has lured you into starting this fight, in which there can be only one loser: our son! What were you thinking of when you began this attack, which could not fail to provoke a defence? Not of the child, I am sure. But of revenge, I suppose? Revenge for what? For my discovery of your guilt?

BARONESS. The child? Were you thinking of the child when you dragged me in the mire before this rabble?

BARON. Helen!— Like wild beasts we have clawed each other bloody. We have laid our disgrace open to all these who take pleasure in our ruin, for in this room we have not a single friend. Our child will after this never be able to speak of his parents as respectable people; he will not be able to start life with a recommendation from father and mother; he will see the home shunned, the old parents isolated and despised, and so the time must come when he will flee us!

BARONESS. What do you want then?

BARON. Let us leave the country after selling the property.

BARONESS. And begin the same squabble all over again! I know what will happen: for a week you will be tame, and then you will abuse me.

BARON. Just think—now they are settling our fate in there. You cannot hope for a good word from the Pastor, whom you have just called a liar; and I, who am known to be no Christian, can expect no mercy either. Oh, I wish I were in the woods, so that I could crawl in under some big roots or put my head under a rock—this is more shame than I can bear!

BARONESS. It is true that the minister hates both of us, and it may happen as you say. Why don't you speak to him?

BARON. Of what? Making up?

BARONESS. Of anything you please, if it only be not too late! Oh, if it should be too late!— What can that man Alexandersson want that makes him prowl about us two all the time? I am afraid of that man!

BARON. Alexandersson is a nice fellow.

BARONESS. Yes, he is nice to you, but not to me— I have observed those glances before— Go and see the Pastor now; but take my hand first— I am scared!

BARON. Of what, dear, of what?

BARONESS. I don't know— Everything, everybody!

BARON. But not of me?

BARONESS. No, not now! It is as if our clothes had been caught in the mill wheels, and we had been dragged into the machinery. What have we been doing? What have we been doing in our anger? How they will enjoy themselves, all these who are now seeing the Baron and the Baroness stripped naked and flogging each other— Oh, I feel as if I were standing here without a rag to cover me

[She buttons her coat.

BARON. Calm yourself, my dear. It is not exactly the proper place to tell you what I have said before: that there is only one friend and one home—but we might start over again!— Well, heaven knows! No, we cannot do it. You have gone too far. It is all over. And this last—yes, let it be the last! And it had to come after all the rest. No, we are enemies for life! And if I let you go away with the child now, then you might marry again— I see that now. And my child might have a step-father; and I should have to watch another man going about with my wife and child— Or I might myself be going about with somebody else's wench hanging on my arm. No! Either you or I! One of us must be struck down! You or I!

BARONESS. You! For if I let you take the child, you might marry again, and I might have to see another woman taking my place with my own child. The mere thought of it could make me a murderess! A step-mother for *my* child!

BARON. You might have thought of it before! But when you saw me champing at the chain of love that bound me to you, then you believed me incapable of loving anybody but yourself.

BARONESS. Do you think I ever loved you?

BARON. Yes, once at least. When I had been faithless to you. Then your love grew sublime. And your pretended scorn made you irresistible. But my error caused you to respect me, too. Whether it was the male or the criminal you admired most, I don't know, but I believe it was both—it must have been both, for you are the most typical woman I have ever met. And now you are already jealous of a new wife whom I have never thought of. What a pity that you became my mate! As my mistress, your victory would have been unchallenged, and your infidelities would only have seemed the bouquet of my new wine.

BARONESS. Yes, your love was always material.

BARON. Material as everything spiritual, and spiritual as all that is material! My weakness for you, which gave strength to my feeling, made you believe yourself the stronger, when you were simply coarser, more ill-natured, and more unscrupulous than I.

BARONESS. You the stronger? You, who never want the same thing two minutes in a stretch! You, who as a rule never know what you want!

BARON. Yes, I know perfectly well what I want, but there is room in me for both love and hatred, and while I love you one minute, I hate you the next. And just now I hate you!

BARONESS. Are you now thinking of the child also?

BARON. Yes, now and always! And do you know why? Because he is our love that has taken flesh. He is the memory of our beautiful hours, the link that unites our souls, the common ground where we must ever meet without wishing to do so. And that is why we shall never be able to part, even if our separation be declared— Oh, if I could only hate you as I want to!

SCENE XI

The JUDGE *and the* PASTOR *enter in conversation and remain in the foreground.*

JUDGE. Thus I recognize the utter hopelessness of seeking justice or discovering truth. And it seems to me as if the laws were a couple of centuries behind our ideas of right. Did I not have to punish Alexandersson, who was innocent, and exonerate the girl, who was guilty of theft? And as for this separation suit, I know nothing at all about it at this minute, and I cannot take upon my conscience to render a decision.

PASTOR. But a decision has to be rendered.

JUDGE. Not by me! I shall give up my place and choose another profession.

PASTOR. Why, such a scandal would only bring you notoriety and close every career to you. Keep on judging a few years, and you will come to think it quite easy to crush human fates like egg shells. And for that matter, if you want to stand clear of this case, let yourself be outvoted by the jury. Then they must take the responsibility on themselves.

JUDGE. That is a way—and I suspect that they will be practically at one against me, for I have formed an opinion in this matter, which, however, is wholly intuitive and, therefore, not to be trusted— I thank you for your advice.

SHERIFF. [*Who has been talking with* ALEXANDERSSON, *steps up to the* JUDGE] In my capacity of public prosecutor, I have to report the farmer Alexandersson as a witness against Baroness Sprengel.

JUDGE. In relation to the adultery charge?

SHERIFF. Yes.

JUDGE. [*To the* PASTOR] Here is a new clue that may lead to a solution.

PASTOR. Oh, there are lots of clues, if you can only get hold of them.

JUDGE. But nevertheless it is horrible to see two persons who have loved trying to ruin each other. It is like being in a slaughter-house!

PASTOR. Well, that is love, Judge!

JUDGE. What then is hatred?

PASTOR. It is the lining of the coat.

       [*The* JUDGE *goes over and speaks to the* JURORS.

BARONESS. [*Comes forward to the* PASTOR] Help us, Pastor! Help us!

PASTOR. I cannot, and as a clergyman, I must not. And furthermore, did I not warn you not to play with such serious matters? You thought it so simple to part! Well, part then! The law will not prevent you, so don't put the blame on it.

SCENE XII

ALL *as before.*

JUDGE. The Court will now resume its proceedings. According to the report of the public prosecutor, Sheriff Wiberg, a new witness has appeared against the Baroness and is ready to affirm her guilt under the charge of adultery. Farmer Alexandersson!

ALEXANDERSSON. I am here.

JUDGE. How can you prove your assertion?

ALEXANDERSSON. I saw the offence committed.

BARONESS. He is lying! Let him bring proof!

ALEXANDERSSON. Proof? I'm a witness now, ain't I?

BARONESS. Your assertion is no proof, although you happen to be called a witness for the moment.

ALEXANDERSSON. Maybe the witness has to have two more witnesses, and those still others?

BARONESS. Yes, it might be needed when one cannot tell whether the whole lot are lying or not.

BARON. The testimony of Alexandersson will not be required. I beg leave to offer the Court all the correspondence by which the marital infidelity of the Baroness stands completely proved— Here are the originals; copies of them will be found in the possession of defendant.

[*The* BARONESS *utters a cry but controls herself quickly.*

JUDGE. And yet, Baroness, you were willing to take the oath a little while ago?

BARONESS. But I didn't take it! And now I think the Baron and I may cry quits.

JUDGE. We do not let one crime cancel another. The account of each one has to be settled separately.

BARONESS. Then I want to file a claim at once against the Baron for my dowry which he has squandered.

JUDGE. If you have squandered your wife's dowry, Baron, it might be well to settle that matter right here.

BARON. The Baroness brought with her six thousand crowns in stock that was then unsalable and soon became wholly worthless. As at the time of our marriage she held a position as a telegrapher and declared herself unwilling to take support from her husband, we made a marriage contract and agreed that each one should be self-supporting. But she lost her position after the marriage, and I have been supporting her ever since. To this I had no objection whatever, but as she is now putting in bills, I shall ask leave to present one of my own to meet hers. It totals up to thirty-five thousand crowns, this being one-third of the household expenses since the beginning of our marriage, and I being willing to take two-thirds upon myself.

JUDGE. Have you this agreement in black and white, Baron ?

BARON. I have not.

JUDGE. Have you any documents to prove the disposition of your dowry, Baroness ?

BARONESS. I didn't think at the time it would be necessary to get anything in writing, as I supposed myself to be dealing with honourable people.

JUDGE. Then this whole question cannot come under consideration here. The jury will please step into the small courtroom for discussion of the case and formulation of a decision.

SCENE XIII

The JURY *and the* JUDGE *go out to the right.*

ALEXANDERSSON. [*To the* SHERIFF] This here justice is more than I can get any sense out of.

SHERIFF. I think it would be wiser for you to go right home now, or you might have the same experience as the farmer from Mariestad. Did you ever hear of it?

ALEXANDERSSON. No.

SHERIFF. Well, he went to court as spectator, was dragged into the case as witness, became a party to it, and ended up with a flogging at the whipping-post.

ALEXANDERSSON. Oh, hell! But I believe it of 'em! I believe anything of 'em!   [*Goes out.*

The BARON *joins the* BARONESS *in the foreground.*

BARONESS You find it hard to keep away from me

BARON. Now I have struck you down, and I am bleeding to death myself, for your blood is mine——

BARONESS And how clever you are at making out bills!

BARON. Only when it comes to counter-claims! Your courage is that of despair, or that of a person sentenced to death. And when you leave here, you will collapse. Then you will no longer be able to load your sorrow and guilt on me, and you will be suffering from remorse. Do you know why I have not killed you?

BARONESS Because you did not dare!

BARON. No! Not even the thought of hell could have held me back—for I don't believe in it. But this was the thought that did it: even if you get the child, you will be gone in five years. That is what the doctor tells me. And then the child

might be left without either father or mother.   Think of it—
all alone in the world!

BARONESS. Five years!— It is a lie!

BARON. In five years!   And then I am left behind with the
child whether you want it or not.

BARONESS. Oh no! For then my family will bring suit to
get the child away from you.   I don't die when I die!

BARON. Evil never dies!   That is so!   But can you explain
why you grudge me the child, and grudge the child me, whom
it needs?   Is it sheer malice—a craving for revenge that
punishes the child? [*The* BARONESS *remains silent*] Do you
know, I remarked to the Pastor that I thought possibly you
might have some doubts concerning the child's parentage,
and that this might be a reason why you would not let me have
the child, lest my happiness be built on a false foundation.
And he replied: No, I don't think her capable of it—not of
such a fine motive— I don't think you know yourself what
makes you so fanatical about this one thing: it is the yearning
for continued existence that goads you into maintaining your
hold.   Our son has your body, but my soul, and that soul you
cannot rid him of.   In him you will have me back when you
least expect it; in him you will find my thoughts, my tastes,
my passions, and for this reason you will hate him one day, as
you hate me now.   That is what I fear!

BARONESS. You seem still a little afraid that he may become mine?

BARON. In your quality of mother and woman, you have
a certain advantage over me with our judges, and although
justice may throw dice blindfolded, there is always a little lead
on one side of each die.

BARONESS. You know how to pay compliments even in the
moment of separation.   Perhaps you don't hate me as much
as you pretend?

BARON. Frankly speaking, I think that I hate not so much you as my dishonour, though you, too, come in for a share. And why this hatred? Perhaps I have overlooked that you are near the forties, and that a masculine element is making its appearance in you. Perhaps it is this element that I notice in your kisses, in your embraces—perhaps that is what I find so repulsive?

BARONESS. Perhaps. For the sorrow of my life has been, as you well know, that I was not born a man.

BARON. Perhaps that became the sorrow of my life! And now you try to avenge yourself on nature for having played with you, and so you want to bring up your son as a woman. Will you promise me one thing?

BARONESS. Will you promise me one thing?

BARON. What is the use of promising?

BARONESS. No, let us give no more promises.

BARON. Will you answer a question truthfully?

BARONESS. If I told the truth, you would think I lied.

BARON. Yes, so I should!

BARONESS. Can you see now that all is over, for ever?

BARON. For ever! It was for ever that we once swore to love each other.

BARONESS. It is too bad that such oaths must be taken!

BARON. Why so? It is always a bond, such as it is.

BARONESS. I never could bear with bonds!

BARON. Do you think it would have been better for us not to bind ourselves?

BARONESS. Better for me, yes.

BARON. I wonder. For then you could not have bound me.

BARONESS. Nor you me.

BARON. And so the result would have been the same—as when you reduce fractions. Consequently: not the law's fault; not our own; not anybody else's. And yet we have

to assume the responsibility! [*The* SHERIFF *approaches*] So!
Now the verdict has been pronounced— Good-bye, Helen!

BARONESS. Good-bye—Axel!

BARON. It is hard to part! And impossible to live together.
But the fight is over at least!

BARONESS. If it were! I fear it is just about to begin.

SHERIFF. The parties will retire while the Court takes
action.

BARONESS. Axel, a word before it is too late! After all,
they might take the child away from both of us. Drive home
and take the boy to your mother, and then we will flee from
here, far away!

BARON. I think you are trying to fool me again.

BARONESS. No, I am not. I am no longer thinking of
you, or of myself, or of my revenge. Save the child only!
Listen, Axel—you must do it!

BARON. I will. But if you are deceiving me— Never
mind: I'll do it!

> *Goes out quickly. The* BARONESS *leaves through the
> door in the background.*

SCENE XIV

The JURY *and the* JUDGE *enter and resume their seats.*

JUDGE. As we now have the case complete before us, I
shall ask each juror separately to state his opinion before
decision is rendered. Personally, I can only hold it reasonable that the child be given to the mother, as both parties
are equally to blame for the estrangement, and as the mother
must be held better adapted to the care of the child than the
father.   [*Silence.*

ALEXANDER EKLUND. According to prevailing law, it is

the wife who takes her rank and condition from the husband, not the husband from the wife.

EMMANUEL WICKBERG. And the husband is the proper guardian of his wife.

CARL JOHAN SJÖBERG. The ritual, which gives binding force to the marriage, says that the wife should obey her husband, and so it is clear to me that the man takes precedence of the woman.

ERIC OTTO BOMAN. And the children are to be brought up in the faith of the father.

ÅRENFRID SÖDERBERG. From which may be concluded that children follow the father and not the mother.

OLOF ANDERSSON OF WIK. But as in the case before us both man and wife are equally guilty, and, judging by what has come to light, equally unfit to rear a child, I hold that the child should be taken away from both.

CARL PETER ANDERSSON OF BERGA. In concurring with Olof Andersson, I may call to mind that in such cases the Court names two good men as guardians to take charge of children and property, so that out of the latter man and wife may have their support together with the child.

AXEL WALLIN. And for guardians I wish in this case to propose Alexander Eklund and Ärenfrid Söderberg, both of whom are well known to be of honest character and Christian disposition.

ANDERS ERIC RUTH. I concur with Olof Andersson of Wik as to the separation of the child from both father and mother, and with Axel Wallin as to the guardians, whose Christian disposition makes them particularly fitted to bring up the child.

SWEN OSCAR ERLING. I concur in what has just been said.

AUGUST ALEXANDER VASS. I concur.

LUDWIG ÖSTMAN. I concur.

JUDGE. As the opinion expressed by a majority of the jurors is contrary to my own, I must ask the Jury to take a vote on the matter. And I think it proper first to put the motion made by Olof Andersson for the separation of the child from both father and mother, and for the appointment of guardians. Is it the unanimous will of the Jury that such action be taken?

ALL THE JURORS. Yes.

JUDGE. If anybody objects to the motion, he will hold up his hand. [*Silence*] The opinion of the Jury has won out against my own, and I shall enter an exception on the minutes against what seems to me the needless cruelty of the decision—   The couple will then be sentenced to a year's separation of bed and board, at the risk of imprisonment if, during that period, they should seek each other. [*To the* SHERIFF] Call in the parties.

SCENE XV

The BARONESS *and* SPECTATORS *enter.*

JUDGE. Is Baron Sprengel not present?

BARONESS. The Baron will be here in a moment.

JUDGE. Whoever does not observe the time, has only himself to blame. This is the decision of the County Court: that husband and wife be sentenced to a year's separation of bed and board, and that the child be taken from the parents and placed in charge of two guardians for education. For this purpose the Court has selected and appointed the jurors Alexander Eklund and Ärenfrid Söderberg.

> *The* BARONESS *cries out and sinks to the floor. The* SHERIFF *and the* CONSTABLE *raise her up and place her on a chair. Some of the* SPECTATORS *leave in the meantime.*

BARON. [*Enters*] Your Honor! I heard the sentence of the Court from the outside, and I wish to enter a challenge, first against the Jury as a whole, it being made up of my personal enemies, and secondly against the guardians, Alexander Eklund and Ärenfrid Söderberg, neither of whom possesses the financial status demanded of guardians. Furthermore, I shall enter proceedings against the judge for incompetence displayed in the exercise of his office, in so far as he has failed to recognise that the primary guilt of one led to the subsequent guilt of the other, so that both cannot be held equally responsible.

JUDGE. Whosoever be not satisfied with the decision rendered may appeal to the higher court within the term set by law. Will the Jury please accompany me on house visitation to the Rectory in connection with the suit pending against the communal assessors?

> *The* JUDGE *and the* JURY *go out through the door in the background.*

SCENE XVI

> *The* BARON *and the* BARONESS. *The* SPECTATORS *withdraw gradually.*

BARONESS. Where is Emil?

BARON. He was gone!

BARONESS. That's a lie!

BARON. [*After a pause*] Yes— I did not bring him to my mother, whom I cannot trust, but to the Rectory.

BARONESS. To the minister!

BARON. Your one reliable enemy! Yes. Who was there else that I might trust? And I did it because a while ago I caught a glance in your eye which made me think that you possibly might kill yourself and the child.

BARONESS. You saw that!— Oh, why did I let myself be fooled into believing you.

BARON. Well, what do you say of all this?

BARONESS. I don't know. But I am so tired that I no longer feel the blows. It seems almost a relief to have received the final stab.

BARON. You give no thought to what is now going to happen: how your son is going to be brought up by two peasants, whose ignorance and rude habits will kill the child by slow torture; how he is going to be forced down into their narrow sphere; how his intelligence is going to be smothered by religious superstition; how he is going to be taught contempt for his father and mother——

BARONESS. Hush! Don't say another word, or I shall lose my reason! My Emil in the hands of peasant women, who don't know enough to wash themselves, who have their beds full of vermin, and who cannot even keep a comb clean! My Emil! No, it is impossible!

BARON. It is the actual reality, and you have nobody but yourself to blame for it.

BARONESS. Myself? But did I make myself? Did I put evil tendencies, hatred, and wild passions into myself? No! And who was it that denied me the power and will to combat all those things?— When I look at myself this moment, I feel that I am to be pitied. Am I not?

BARON. Yes, you are! Both of us are to be pitied. We tried to avoid the rocks that beset marriage by living unmarried as husband and wife; but nevertheless we quarrelled, and we were sacrificing one of life's greatest joys, the respect of our fellow-men—and so we were married. But we must needs steal a march on the social body and its laws. We wanted no religious ceremony, but instead we wriggled into a civil marriage. We did not want to depend on each other—we were to have no common pocket-book and to insist on no personal ownership of each other—and with that we fell right back into the old rut again. Without wedding ceremony, but with a marriage contract! And then it went to pieces. I forgave your faithlessness, and for the child's sake we lived together in voluntary separation—and freedom! But I grew tired of introducing my friend's mistress as my wife—and so we had to get a divorce. Can you guess—do you know against whom we have been fighting? You call him God, but I call him nature. And that was the master who egged us on to hate each other, just as he is egging people on to love each other. And now we are condemned to keep on tearing each other as long as a spark of life remains. New proceedings in the higher court, reopening of the case, report by the Vestry Board, opinion from the Diocesan Chapter, decision by the Supreme Court. Then comes my complaint to the Attorney-General, my application for a guardian, your objections and counter-suits: from pillory to post! Without hope of a merciful executioner! Neglect of the property, financial ruin, scamped education for the child! And why do we not put an end to these two miserable lives? Because the child stays our hands! You cry, but I cannot! Not even when my thought runs ahead to the night that is waiting for me in a home laid waste! And you, poor Helen, who must go back to your mother! That mother whom you once left with such eagerness in order to get a home of your own. To become her daughter once more—and perhaps find it worse than being a wife! One year! Two years! Many years! How many more do you think we can bear to suffer?

BARONESS. I shall never go back to my mother. Never! I shall go out on the high-roads and into the woods so that I may find a hiding-place where I can scream—scream myself tired against God, who has put this infernal love into the world as a torment for us human creatures—and when night comes, I shall seek shelter in the Pastor's barn, so that I may sleep near my child.

BARON. You hope to sleep to-night—you?

Curtain.

THE DANCE OF DEATH

1901

PART I

CHARACTERS

EDGAR, *Captain in the Coast Artillery*
ALICE, *his wife, a former actress*
CURT, *Master of Quarantine*
JENNY
THE OLD WOMAN   } *Subordinate characters*
THE SENTRY

THE DANCE OF DEATH

PART I

The scene is laid inside of a round fort built of granite.

In the background, a gateway, closed by huge, swinging double doors; in these, small square window panes, through which may be seen a sea shore with batteries and the sea beyond.

On either side of the gateway, a window with flower pots and bird cages.

To the right of the gateway, an upright piano; further down the stage, a sewing-table and two easy-chairs.

On the left, half-way down the stage, a writing-table with a telegraph instrument on it: further down, a what-not full of framed photographs. Beside it, a couch that can be used to sleep on. Against the wall, a buffet.

A lamp suspended from the ceiling. On the wall near the piano hang two large laurel wreaths with ribbons. Between them, the picture of a woman in stage dress.

Beside the door, a hat-stand on which hang accoutrements, sabres, and so forth. Near it, a chiffonier.

To the left of the gateway hangs a mercurial barometer.

It is a mild Fall evening. The doors stand open, and a sentry is seen pacing back and forth on the shore battery. He wears a helmet with a forward pointed brush for a crest. Now and then his drawn sabre catches the red glare of the setting sun. The sea lies dark and quiet.

> *The CAPTAIN sits in the easy-chair to the left of the sewing-table, fumbling an extinguished cigar. He has on a much-worn undress uniform and riding-boots with spurs. Looks tired and bored.*

> *ALICE sits in the easy-chair on the right, doing nothing at all. Looks tired and expectant.*

CAPTAIN. Won't you play something for me?

ALICE. [*Indifferently, but not snappishly*] What am I to play?

CAPTAIN. Whatever suits you.

ALICE. You don't like my repertory.

CAPTAIN. Nor you mine.

ALICE. [*Evasively*] Do you want the doors to stay open?

CAPTAIN. If you wish it.

ALICE. Let them be, then.   [*Pause*] Why don't you smoke?

CAPTAIN. Strong tobacco is beginning not to agree with me.

ALICE. [*In an almost friendly tone*] Get weaker tobacco
    then.   It is your only pleasure, as you call it.

CAPTAIN. Pleasure—what is that?

ALICE. Don't ask me.   I know it as little as you—   Don't
you want your whiskey yet?

CAPTAIN. I'll wait a little.   What have you for supper?

ALICE. How do I know?   Ask Christine.

CAPTAIN. The mackerel ought to be in season soon—now
the Fall is here.

ALICE. Yes, it is Fall!

CAPTAIN. Within and without.   But leaving aside the cold
that comes with the Fall, both within and without, a little
broiled mackerel, with a slice of lemon and a glass of white
Burgundy, wouldn't be so very bad.

ALICE. Now you grow eloquent.

CAPTAIN. Have we any Burgundy left in the wine-cellar?

ALICE. So far as I know, we have had no wine-cellar these
last five years——

CAPTAIN. You never know anything.   However, we *must*
stock up for our silver wedding.

ALICE. Do you actually mean to celebrate it?

CAPTAIN. Of course!

ALICE. It would be more seemly to hide our misery—our twenty-five years of misery——

CAPTAIN. My dear Alice, it has been a misery, but we have also had some fun—now and then. One has to avail one-self of what little time there is, for afterward it is all over.

ALICE. Is it over? Would that it were!

CAPTAIN. It is over! Nothing left but what can be put on a wheel-barrow and spread on the garden beds.

ALICE. And so much trouble for the sake of the garden beds!

CAPTAIN. Well, that's the way of it. And it is not of my making.

ALICE. So much trouble! [*Pause*] Did the mail come?

CAPTAIN. Yes.

ALICE. Did the butcher send his bill?

CAPTAIN. Yes.

ALICE. How large is it?

CAPTAIN. [*Takes a paper from his pocket and puts on his spectacles, but takes them off again at once*] Look at it yourself. I cannot see any longer.

ALICE. What is wrong with your eyes?

CAPTAIN. Don't know.

ALICE. Growing old?

CAPTAIN. Nonsense! I?

ALICE. Well, not I!

CAPTAIN. Hm!

ALICE. [*Looking at the bill*] Can you pay it?

CAPTAIN. Yes, but not this moment.

ALICE. Some other time, of course! In a year, when you have been retired with a small pension, and it is too late! And then, when your trouble returns——

CAPTAIN. Trouble? I never had any trouble—only a slight indisposition once. And I can live another twenty years.

ALICE. The doctor thought otherwise.

CAPTAIN. The doctor!

ALICE. Yes, who else could express any valid opinion about sickness?

CAPTAIN. I have no sickness, and never had. I am not going to have it either, for I shall die all of a sudden—like an old soldier.

ALICE. Speaking of the doctor—you know they are having a party to-night?

CAPTAIN. [*Agitated*] Yes, what of it? We are not invited because we don't associate with those people, and we don't associate with them because we don't want to—because we despise both of them. Rabble—that's what they are!

ALICE. You say that of everybody.

CAPTAIN. Because everybody is rabble.

ALICE. Except yourself.

CAPTAIN. Yes, because I have behaved decently under all conditions of life. That's why I don't belong to the rabble.

[*Pause.*

ALICE. Do you want to play cards?

CAPTAIN. All right.

ALICE. [*Takes a pack of cards from the drawer in the sewing-table and begins to shuffle them*] Just think, the doctor is permitted to use the band for a private entertainment!

CAPTAIN. [*Angrily*] That's because he goes to the city and truckles to the Colonel. Truckle, you know—if one could only do that!

ALICE. [*Deals*] I used to be friendly with Gerda, but she played me false——

CAPTAIN. They are all false! What did you turn up for trumps?

ALICE. Put on your spectacles.

CAPTAIN. They are no help— Well, well!

ALICE. Spades are trumps.

CAPTAIN. [*Disappointed*] Spades——?

ALICE. [*Leads*] Well, be that as it may, our case is settled in advance with the wives of the new officers.

CAPTAIN. [*Taking the trick*] What does it matter? We never give any parties anyhow, so nobody is the wiser. I can live by myself—as I have always done.

ALICE. I, too. But the children? The children have to grow up without any companionship.

CAPTAIN. Let them find it for themselves in the city— I take that! Got any trumps left?

ALICE. One— That's mine!

CAPTAIN. Six and eight make fifteen——

ALICE. Fourteen—fourteen!

CAPTAIN. Six and eight make fourteen. I think I am also forgetting how to count. And two makes sixteen— [*Yawns*] It is your deal.

ALICE. You are tired?

CAPTAIN. [*Dealing*] Not at all.

ALICE. [*Listening in direction of the open doors*] One can hear the music all this way. [*Pause*] Do you think Curt is invited also?

CAPTAIN. He arrived this morning, so I guess he has had time to get out his evening clothes, though he has not had time to call on us.

ALICE. Master of Quarantine—is there to be a quarantine station here?

CAPTAIN. Yes.

ALICE. He is my own cousin after all, and once I bore the same name as he——

CAPTAIN. In which there was no particular honour——

ALICE. See here! [*Sharply*] You leave my family alone, and I'll leave yours!

CAPTAIN. All right, all right—don't let us begin again!

ALICE. Must the Master of Quarantine be a physician?

CAPTAIN. Oh, no, he's merely a sort of superintendent or book-keeper—and Curt never became anything in particular.

ALICE. He was not much good——

CAPTAIN. And he has cost us a lot of money. And when he left wife and children, he became disgraced.

ALICE. Not quite so severe, Edgar!

CAPTAIN. That's what happened! What has he been doing in America since then? Well, I cannot say that I am longing for him—but he was a nice chap, and I liked to argue with him.

ALICE. Because he was so tractable——

CAPTAIN. [*Haughtily*] Tractable or not, he was at least a man one could talk to. Here, on this island, there is not *one* person who understands what I say—it's a community of idiots!

ALICE. It is rather strange that Curt should arrive just in time for our silver wedding—whether we celebrate it or not——

CAPTAIN. Why is that strange? Oh, I see! It was he who brought us together, or got you married, as they put it.

ALICE. Well, didn't he?

CAPTAIN. Certainly! It was a kind of fixed idea with him— I leave it for you to say what kind.

ALICE. A wanton fancy——

CAPTAIN. For which we have had to pay, and not he!

ALICE. Yes, think only if I had remained on the stage! All my friends are stars now.

CAPTAIN. [*Rising*] Well, well, well! Now I am going to have a drink [*Goes over to the buffet and mixes a drink, which he takes standing up*] There should be a rail here to put the foot on, so that one might dream of being at Copenhagen, in the American Bar.

ALICE. Let us put a rail there, if it will only remind us of Copenhagen. For there we spent our best moments.

CAPTAIN. [*Drinks quickly*] Yes, do you remember that "navarin aux pommes"?

ALICE. No, but I remember the concerts at the Tivoli.

CAPTAIN. Yes, your tastes are so—exalted!

ALICE. It ought to please you to have a wife whose taste is good.

CAPTAIN. So it does.

ALICE. Sometimes, when you need something to brag of——

CAPTAIN. [*Drinking*] I guess they must be dancing at the doctor's—I catch the three-four time of the tuba: boom—boom-boom!

ALICE. I can hear the entire melody of the Alcazar Waltz. Well, it was not yesterday I danced a waltz——

CAPTAIN. You think you could still manage?

ALICE. Still?

CAPTAIN. Ye-es. I guess you are done with dancing, you like me!

ALICE. I am ten years younger than you.

CAPTAIN. Then we are of the same age, as the lady should be ten years younger.

ALICE. Be ashamed of yourself! You are an old man—and I am still in my best years.

CAPTAIN. Oh, I know, you can be quite charming—to others, when you make up your mind to it.

ALICE. Can we light the lamp now?

CAPTAIN. Certainly.

ALICE. Will you ring, please.

> The CAPTAIN *goes languidly to the writing-table and rings a bell.*
>
> JENNY *enters from the right.*

CAPTAIN. Will you be kind enough to light the lamp, Jenny?

ALICE. [*Sharply*] I want you to light the hanging lamp.

JENNY. Yes, ma'am.

> [*Lights the lamp while the* CAPTAIN *watches her.*

ALICE. [*Stiffly*] Did you wipe the chimney?

JENNY. Sure.

ALICE. What kind of an answer is that?

CAPTAIN. Now—now——

ALICE. [*To* JENNY] Leave us. I will light the lamp myself. That will be better.

JENNY. I think so too.   [*Starts for the door.*

ALICE. [*Rising*] Go!

JENNY. [*Stops*] I wonder, ma'am, what you'd say if I did go?

> ALICE *remains silent.*
>
> JENNY *goes out.*
>
> The CAPTAIN *comes forward and lights the lamp.*

ALICE. [*With concern*] Do you think she will go?

CAPTAIN. Shouldn't wonder. And then we are in for it——

ALICE. It's your fault! You spoil them.

CAPTAIN. Not at all. Can't you see that they are always polite to me?

ALICE. Because you cringe to them. And you always cringe to inferiors, for that matter, because, like all despots, you have the nature of a slave.

CAPTAIN. There—there!

ALICE. Yes, you cringe before your men, and before your sergeants, but you cannot get on with your equals or your superiors.

CAPTAIN. Ugh!

ALICE. That's the way of all tyrants— Do you think she will go?

CAPTAIN. Yes, if you don't go out and say something nice to her.

ALICE. I?

CAPTAIN. Yes, for if I should do it, you would say that I was flirting with the maids.

ALICE. Mercy, if she should leave! Then I shall have to do the work, as I did the last time, and my hands will be spoiled.

CAPTAIN. That is not the worst of it. But if Jenny leaves, Christine will also leave, and then we shall never get a servant to the island again. The mate on the steamer scares away every one that comes to look for a place—and if he should miss his chance, then my corporals attend to it.

ALICE. Yes, your corporals, whom I have to feed in my kitchen, and whom you dare not show the door——

CAPTAIN. No, for then they would also go when their terms were up—and we might have to close up the whole gun shop!

ALICE. It will be our ruin.

CAPTAIN. That's why the officers have proposed to petition His Royal Majesty for special expense money.

ALICE. For whom?

CAPTAIN. For the corporals.

ALICE. [Laughing] You are crazy!

CAPTAIN. Yes, laugh a little for me. I need it.

ALICE. I shall soon have forgotten how to laugh——

CAPTAIN. [Lighting his cigar] That is something one should never forget—it is tedious enough anyhow!

ALICE. Well, it is not very amusing— Do you want to play any more?

CAPTAIN. No, it tires me.   [Pause.

ALICE. Do you know, it irritates me nevertheless that my cousin, the new Master of Quarantine, makes his first visit to our enemies.

CAPTAIN. Well, what's the use of talking about it?

ALICE. But did you see in the paper that he was put down as *rentier*? He must have come into some money then.

CAPTAIN. *Rentier!* Well, well—a rich relative. That's really the first one in this family.

ALICE. In your family, yes. But among my people many have been rich.

CAPTAIN. If he has money, he's conceited, I suppose, but I'll hold him in check—and he won't get a chance to look at my cards.

The telegraph receiver begins to click.

ALICE. Who is it?

CAPTAIN. [*Standing still*] Keep quiet, please.

ALICE. Well, are you not going to look——

CAPTAIN. I can hear—I can hear what they are saying— It's the children.

Goes over to the instrument and sends an answer; the receiver continues to click for awhile, and then the CAPTAIN answers again.

ALICE. Well?

CAPTAIN. Wait a little— [*Gives a final click*] The children are at the guard-house in the city. Judith is not well again and is staying away from school.

ALICE. Again! What more did they say?

CAPTAIN. Money, of course!

ALICE. Why is Judith in such a hurry? If she didn't pass her examinations until next year, it would be just as well.

CAPTAIN. Tell her, and see what it helps.

ALICE. You should tell her.

CAPTAIN. How many times have I not done so? But children have their own wills, you know.

ALICE. Yes, in this house at least. [*The CAPTAIN yawns*] So, you yawn in your wife's presence!

CAPTAIN. Well, what can I do? Don't you notice how day by day we are saying the same things to each other? When, just now, you sprang that good old phrase of yours, "in this house at least," I should have come back with my own stand-by, "it is not my house only." But as I have already made that reply some five hundred times, I yawned instead. And my yawn could be taken to mean either that I was too lazy to answer, or "right you are, my angel," or "supposing we quit."

ALICE. You are very amiable to-night.

CAPTAIN. Is it not time for supper soon?

ALICE. Do you know that the doctor ordered supper from the city—from the Grand Hotel?

CAPTAIN. No! Then they are having ptarmigans—tschk! Ptarmigan, you know, is the finest bird there is, but it's clear barbarism to fry it in bacon grease——

ALICE. Ugh! Don't talk of food.

CAPTAIN. Well, how about wines? I wonder what those barbarians are drinking with the ptarmigans?

ALICE. Do you want me to play for you?

CAPTAIN. [Sits down at the writing-table] The last resource! Well, if you could only leave your dirges and lamentations alone—it sounds too much like music with a moral. And I am always adding within myself: "Can't you hear how unhappy I am! Meow, meow! Can't you hear what a horrible husband I have! Brum, brum, brum! If he would only die soon! Beating of the joyful drum, flourishes, the finale of the Alcazar Waltz, Champagne Galop!" Speaking of champagne, I guess there are a couple of bottles left. What would you say about bringing them up and pretending to have company?

ALICE. No, we won't, for they are mine—they were given to me personally.

CAPTAIN. You are so economical.

ALICE. And you are always stingy—to your wife at least!

CAPTAIN. Then I don't know what to suggest.   Perhaps I might dance for you?

ALICE. No, thank you—I guess you are done with dancing.

CAPTAIN. You should bring some friend to stay with you.

ALICE. Thanks! You might bring a friend to stay with you.

CAPTAIN. Thanks! It has been tried, and with mutual dissatisfaction.   But it was interesting in the way of an experiment, for as soon as a stranger entered the house, we became quite happy—to begin with——

ALICE. And then!

CAPTAIN. Oh, don't talk of it!

There is a knock at the door on the left.

ALICE. Who can be coming so late as this?

CAPTAIN. Jenny does not knock.

ALICE. Go and open the door, and don't yell "come"— it has a sound of the workshop.

CAPTAIN. [*Goes toward the door on the left*] You don't like workshops.

ALICE. Please, open!

CAPTAIN. [*Opens the door and receives a visiting-card that is held out to him*] It is Christine— Has Jenny left? [*As the public cannot hear the answer, to* ALICE] Jenny has left.

ALICE. Then I become servant girl again!

CAPTAIN. And I man-of-all-work.

ALICE. Would it not be possible to get one of your gunners to help along in the kitchen?

. CAPTAIN. Not these days.

ALICE. But it couldn't be Jenny who sent in her card?

CAPTAIN. [*Looks at the card through his spectacles and then turns it over to* ALICE] You see what it is—I cannot.

ALICE. [*Looks at the card*] Curt—it is Curt! Hurry up and bring him in.

CAPTAIN. [*Goes out to the left*] Curt! Well, that's a pleasure!

[ALICE *arranges her hair and seems to come to life.*

CAPTAIN. [*Enters from the left with* CURT] Here he is, the traitor! Welcome, old man! Let me hug you!

ALICE. [*Goes to* CURT] Welcome to my home, Curt!

CURT. Thank you—it is some time since we saw each other.

CAPTAIN. How long? Fifteen years! And we have grown old——

ALICE. Oh, Curt has not changed, it seems to me.

CAPTAIN. Sit down, sit down! And first of all—the programme. Have you any engagement for to-night?

CURT. I am invited to the doctor's, but I have not promised to go.

ALICE. Then you will stay with your relatives.

CURT. That would seem the natural thing, but the doctor is my superior, and I might have trouble afterward.

CAPTAIN. What kind of talk is that? I have never been afraid of my superiors——

CURT. Fear or no fear, the trouble cannot be escaped.

CAPTAIN. On this island I am master. Keep behind my back, and nobody will dare to touch you.

ALICE. Oh, be quiet, Edgar! [*Takes* CURT *by the hand*] Leaving both masters and superiors aside, you must stay with us. That will be found both natural and proper.

CURT. Well, then—especially as I feel welcome here.

CAPTAIN. Why should you not be welcome? There is nothing between us— [CURT *tries vainly to hide a sense of displeasure*] What could there be? You were a little careless as a young man, but I have forgotten all about it. I don't let things rankle.

ALICE *looks annoyed. All three sit down at the sewing-table.*

ALICE. Well, you have strayed far and wide in the world?

CURT. Yes, and now I have found a harbour with you——

CAPTAIN. Whom you married off twenty-five years ago.

CURT. It was not quite that way, but it doesn't matter. It is pleasing to see that you have stuck together for twenty-five years.

CAPTAIN. Well, we have borne with it. Now and then it has been so-so, but, as you say, we have stuck together. And Alice has had nothing to complain of. There has been plenty of everything—heaps of money. Perhaps you don't know that I am a celebrated author—an author of text-books——

CURT. Yes, I recall that, when we parted, you had just published a volume on rifle practice that was selling well. Is it still used in the military schools?

CAPTAIN. It is still in evidence, and it holds its place as number one, though they have tried to substitute a worse one—which is being used now, but which is totally worthless.

[*Painful silence.*]

CURT. You have been travelling abroad, I have heard.

ALICE. We have been down to Copenhagen five times—think of it?

CAPTAIN. Well, you see, when I took Alice away from the stage——

ALICE. Oh, you took me?

CAPTAIN. Yes, I took you as a wife should be taken——

ALICE. How brave you have grown!

CAPTAIN. But as it was held up against me afterward that I had spoiled her brilliant career—hm!—I had to make up for it by promising to take my wife to Copenhagen—and this I have kept—fully! Five times we have been there. Five [*holding up the five fingers of the left hand*] Have you been in Copenhagen?

CURT. [*Smiling*] No, I have mostly been in America.

CAPTAIN. America? Isn't that a rotten sort of a country?

CURT. [*Unpleasantly impressed*] It is not Copenhagen.

ALICE. Have you—heard anything—from your children?

CURT. No.

ALICE. I hope you pardon me—but was it not rather inconsiderate to leave them like that——

CURT. I didn't leave them, but the court gave them to the mother.

CAPTAIN. Don't let us talk of that now. I for my part think it was lucky for you to get out of that mess.

CURT. [*To* ALICE] How are your children?

ALICE. Well, thank you. They are at school in the city and will soon be grown up.

CAPTAIN. Yes, they're splendid kids, and the boy has a brilliant head—brilliant! He is going to join the General Staff——

ALICE. If they accept him!

CAPTAIN. Him? Who has the making of a War Minister in him!

CURT. From one thing to another. There is to be a quarantine station here—against plague, cholera, and that sort of thing. And the doctor will be my superior, as you know—what sort of man is he?

CAPTAIN. Man? He is no man! He's an ignorant rascal!

CURT. [*To* ALICE] That is very unpleasant for me.

ALICE. Oh, it is not quite as bad as Edgar makes it out, but I must admit that I have small sympathy for the man——

CAPTAIN. A rascal, that's what he is. And that's what the others are, too—the Collector of Customs, the Postmaster, the telephone girl, the druggist, the pilot—what is it they call him now?—the Pilot Master—rascals one and all—and that's why I don't associate with them.

CURT. Are you on bad terms with all of them?

CAPTAIN. Every one!

ALICE. Yes, it is true that intercourse with those people is out of the question.

CAPTAIN. It is as if all the tyrants of the country had been sent to this island for safe-keeping.

ALICE. [*Ironically*] Exactly!

CAPTAIN. [*Good-naturedly*] Hm! Is that meant for me? I am no tyrant—not in my own house at least.

ALICE. You know better!

CAPTAIN. [*To* CURT] Don't believe her! I am a very reasonable husband, and the old lady is the best wife in the world.

ALICE. Would you like something to drink, Curt?

CURT. No, thank you, not now.

CAPTAIN. Have you turned——

CURT. A little moderate only——

CAPTAIN. Is that American?

CURT. Yes.

CAPTAIN. No moderation for me, or I don't care at all. A man should stand his liquor.

CURT. Returning to our neighbours on the island—my position will put me in touch with all of them—and it is not easy to steer clear of everything, for no matter how little you care to get mixed up in other people's intrigues, you are drawn into them just the same.

ALICE. You had better take up with them—in the end you will return to us, for here you find your true friends.

CURT. Is it not dreadful to be alone among a lot of enemies as you are?

ALICE. It is not pleasant.

CAPTAIN. It isn't dreadful at all. I have never had anything but enemies all my life, and they have helped me on instead of doing me harm. And when my time to die comes,

I may say that I owe nothing to anybody, and that I have never got a thing for nothing. Every particle of what I own I have had to fight for.

ALICE. Yes, Edgar's path has not been strewn with roses——

CAPTAIN. No, with thorns and stones—pieces of flint—but a man's own strength: do you know what that means?

CURT. [Simply] Yes, I learned to recognise its insufficiency about ten years ago.

CAPTAIN. Then you are no good!

ALICE. [To the CAPTAIN] Edgar!

CAPTAIN. He is no good, I say, if he does not have the strength within himself. Of course it is true that when the mechanism goes to pieces there is nothing left but a barrow-ful to chuck out on the garden beds; but as long as the mechanism holds together the thing to do is to kick and fight, with hands and feet, until there is nothing left. That is my philosophy.

CURT. [Smiling] It is fun to listen to you.

CAPTAIN. But you don't think it's true?

CURT. No, I don't.

CAPTAIN. But true it is, for all that.

> During the preceding scene the wind has begun to blow hard, and now one of the big doors is closed with a bang.

CAPTAIN. [Rising] It's blowing. I could just feel it coming.

> Goes back and closes both doors. Knocks on the barometer.

ALICE. [To CURT] You will stay for supper?

CURT. Thank you.

ALICE. But it will be very simple, as our housemaid has just left us.

CURT. Oh, it will do for me, I am sure.

ALICE. You ask for so little, dear Curt.

CAPTAIN. [*At the barometer*] If you could only see how the mercury is dropping! Oh, I felt it coming!

ALICE. [*Secretly to* CURT] He is nervous.

CAPTAIN. We ought to have supper soon.

ALICE. [*Rising*] I am going to see about it now. You can sit here and philosophise—[*secretly to* CURT], but don't contradict him, for then he gets into bad humour. And don't ask him why he was not made a major.

[CURT *nods assent.*

[ALICE *goes toward the right.*

CAPTAIN. See that we get something nice now, old lady!

ALICE. You give me money, and you'll get what you want.

CAPTAIN. Always money!

[ALICE *goes out.*

CAPTAIN. [*To* CURT] Money, money, money! All day long I have to stand ready with the purse, until at last I have come to feel as if I myself were nothing but a purse. Are you familiar with that kind of thing?

CURT. Oh, yes—with the difference that I took myself for a pocket-book.

CAPTAIN. Ha-ha! So you know the flavour of the brand! Oh, the ladies! Ha-ha! And you had one of the proper kind!

CURT. [*Patiently*] Let that be buried now.

CAPTAIN. She was a jewel! Then I have after all—in spite of everything—one that's pretty decent. For she is straight, in spite of everything.

CURT. [*Smiling good-humouredly*] In spite of everything.

CAPTAIN. Don't you laugh!

CURT. [*As before*] In spite of everything!

CAPTAIN. Yes, she has been a faithful mate, a splendid mother—excellent—but [*with a glance at the door on the right*] she has a devilish temper. Do you know, there have been moments when I cursed you for saddling me with her.

Curt. [*Good-naturedly*] But I didn't.   Listen, man——

Captain. Yah, yah, yah! You talk nonsense and forget things that are not pleasant to remember. Don't take it badly, please— I am accustomed to command and raise Cain, you see, but you know me, and don't get angry!

Curt. Not at all. But I have not provided you with a wife—on the contrary.

Captain. [*Without letting his flow of words be checked*] Don't you think life is queer anyhow?

Curt. I suppose so.

Captain. And to grow old—it is no fun, but it is interesting. Well, my age is nothing to speak of, but it does begin to make itself felt. All your friends die off, and then you become so lonely.

Curt. Lucky the man who can grow old in company with a wife.

Captain. Lucky? Well, it is luck, for the children go their way, too. You ought not to have left yours.

Curt. Well, I didn't. They were taken away from me——

Captain. Don't get mad now, because I tell you——

Curt. But it was not so.

Captain. Well, whichever way it was, it has now become forgotten—but you are alone!

Curt. You get accustomed to everything.

Captain. Do you—is it possible to get accustomed—to being quite alone also?

Curt. Here am I!

Captain. What have you been doing these fifteen years?

Curt. What a question! These fifteen years!

Captain. They say you have got hold of money and grown rich.

Curt. I can hardly be called rich——

Captain. I am not going to ask for a loan.

CURT. If you were, you would find me ready.

CAPTAIN. Many thanks, but I have my bank account. You see [*with a glance toward the door on the right*], nothing must be lacking in this house; and the day I had no more money—she would leave me!

CURT. Oh, no!

CAPTAIN. No? Well, I know better. Think of it, she makes a point of asking me when I happen to be short, just for the pleasure of showing me that I am not supporting my family.

CURT. But I heard you say that you have a large income.

CAPTAIN. Of course, I have a large income—but it is not enough.

CURT. Then it is not large, as such things are reckoned——

CAPTAIN. Life is queer, and we as well!

The telegraph receiver begins to click.

CURT. What is that?

CAPTAIN. Nothing but a time correction.

CURT. Have you no telephone?

CAPTAIN. Yes, in the kitchen. But we use the telegraph because the girls at the central report everything we say.

CURT. Social conditions out here by the sea must be frightful!

CAPTAIN. They are simply horrible! But all life is horrible. And you, who believe in a sequel, do you think there will be any peace further on?

CURT. I presume there will be storms and battles there also.

CAPTAIN. There also—if there be any "there"! I prefer annihilation!

CURT. Are you sure that annihilation will come without pain?

CAPTAIN. I am going to die all of a sudden, without pain.

CURT. So you know that?

CAPTAIN. Yes, I know it.

CURT. You don't appear satisfied with your life?

CAPTAIN. [*Sighing*] Satisfied? The day I could die, I should be satisfied.

CURT. [*Rising*] That you don't know! But tell me: what is going on in this house? What is happening here? There is a smell as of poisonous wall-paper, and one feels sick the moment one enters. I should prefer to get away from here, had I not promised Alice to stay. There are dead bodies beneath the flooring, and the place is so filled with hatred that one can hardly breathe. [*The* CAPTAIN *sinks together and sits staring into vacancy*] What is the matter with you? Edgar! [*The* CAPTAIN *does not move. Slaps the* CAPTAIN *on the shoulder*] Edgar!

CAPTAIN. [*Recovering consciousness*] Did you say anything? [*Looks around*] I thought it was—Alice!— Oh, is that you?— Say—   [*Relapses into apathy.*

CURT. This is horrible! [*Goes over to the door on the right and opens it*] Alice!

ALICE. [*Enters, wearing a kitchen apron*] What is it?

CURT. I don't know. Look at him.

ALICE. [*Calmly*] He goes off like that at times— I'll play and then he will wake up.

CURT. No, don't! Not that way! Leave it to me— Does he hear? Or see?

ALICE. Just now he neither hears nor sees.

CURT. And you can speak of that with such calm? Alice, what is going on in this house?

ALICE. Ask him there.

CURT. Him there? But he is your husband!

ALICE. A stranger to me—as strange as he was twenty-five years ago. I know nothing at all about that man—nothing but——

CURT. Stop!   He may overhear you.

ALICE. Now he cannot hear anything.

A trumpet signal is sounded outside.

CAPTAIN. [*Leaps to his feet and grabs sabre and cap*] Pardon me.   I have to inspect the sentries.

[*Goes out through the door in the background.*

CURT. Is he ill?

ALICE. I don't know.

CURT. Has he lost his reason?

ALICE. I don't know.

CURT. Does he drink?

ALICE. He boasts more of it than he really drinks.

CURT. Sit down and talk—but calmly and truthfully.

ALICE. [*Sitting down*] What am I to talk about?   That I have spent a lifetime in this tower, locked up, guarded by a man whom I have always hated, and whom I now hate so beyond all bounds that the day he died I should be laughing until the air shook.

CURT. Why have you not parted?

ALICE. You may well ask!   While still engaged we parted twice; since then we have been trying to part every single day —but we are chained together and cannot break away.   Once we were separated—within the same house—for five whole years.   Now nothing but death can part us.   This we know, and for that reason we are waiting for him as for a liberator.

CURT. Why are you so lonely?

ALICE. Because he isolates me.   First he "exterminated" all my brothers and sisters from our home—he speaks of it himself as "extermination"—and then my girl friends and everybody else.

CURT. But *his* relatives?   He has not "exterminated" them?

ALICE. Yes, for they came near taking my life, after having taken my honour and good name.   Finally I became forced to keep up my connection with the world and with other human beings by means of that telegraph—for the telephone was watched by the operators. I have taught myself telegraphy, and he doesn't know it. You must not tell him, for then he would kill me.

CURT. Frightful! Frightful!— But why does he hold me responsible for your marriage? Let me tell you now how it was. Edgar was my childhood friend. When he saw you he fell in love at once. He came to me and asked me to plead his cause. I said no at once—and, my dear Alice, I knew your tyrannical and cruel temperament. For that reason I warned him—and when he persisted, I sent him to get your brother for his spokesman.

ALICE. I believe what you say. But he has been deceiving himself all these years, so that now you can never get him to believe anything else.

CURT. Well, let him put the blame on me if that can relieve his sufferings.

ALICE. But that is too much——

CURT. I am used to it. But what does hurt me is his unjust charge that I have deserted my children——

ALICE. That's the manner of man he is. He says what suits him, and then he believes it. But he seems to be fond of you, principally because you don't contradict him. Try not to grow tired of us now. I believe you have come in what was to us a fortunate moment; I think it was even providential— Curt, you must not grow tired of us, for we are undoubtedly the most unhappy creatures in the whole world!

[*She weeps.*

CURT. I have seen *one* marriage at close quarters, and it was dreadful—but this is almost worse!

ALICE. Do you think so?

CURT. Yes.

ALICE. Whose fault is it?

CURT. The moment you quit asking whose fault it is, Alice, you will feel a relief.   Try to regard it as a fact, a trial that has to be borne——

ALICE. I cannot do it! It is too much! [*Rising*] It is beyond help!

CURT. I pity both of you!— Do you know why you are hating each other?

ALICE. No, it is the most unreasoning hatred, without cause, without purpose, but also without end. And can you imagine why he is principally afraid of death? He fears that I may marry again.

CURT. Then he loves you.

ALICE. Probably. But that does not prevent him from hating me.

CURT. [*As if to himself*] It is called love-hatred, and it hails from the pit!— Does he like you to play for him?

ALICE. Yes, but only horrid melodies—for instance, that awful "The Entry of the Boyars." When he hears it he loses his head and wants to dance.

CURT. Does he dance?

ALICE. Oh, he is very funny at times.

CURT. One thing—pardon me for asking. Where are the children?

ALICE. Perhaps you don't know that two of them are dead?

CURT. So you have had that to face also?

ALICE. What is there I have not faced?

CURT. But the other two?

ALICE. In the city. They couldn't stay at home. For he set them against me.

CURT. And you set them against him?

ALICE. Of course. And then parties were formed, votes bought, bribes given—and in order not to spoil the children completely we had to part from them. What should have been the uniting link became the seed of dissension; what is held the blessing of the home turned into a curse—well, I believe sometimes that we belong to a cursed race!

CURT. Yes, is it not so—ever since the Fall?

ALICE. [*With a venomous glance and sharp voice*] What fall?

CURT. That of our first parents.

ALICE. Oh, I thought you meant something else!

[*Embarrassed silence.*

ALICE. [*With folded hands*] Curt, my kinsman, my childhood friend—I have not always acted toward you as I should. But now I am being punished, and you are having your revenge.

CURT. No revenge! Nothing of that kind here! Hush!

ALICE. Do you recall one Sunday while you were engaged— and I had invited you for dinner——

CURT. Never mind!

ALICE. I must speak! Have pity on me! When you came to dinner, we had gone away, and you had to leave again.

CURT. You had received an invitation yourselves—what is that to speak of!

ALICE. Curt, when to-day, a little while ago, I asked you to stay for supper, I thought we had something left in the pantry. [*Hiding her face in her hands*] And there is not a thing, not even a piece of bread——

CURT. [*Weeping*] Alice—poor Alice!

ALICE. But when he comes home and wants something to eat, and there is nothing—then he gets angry. You have never seen him angry! O, God, what humiliation!

CURT. Will you not let me go out and arrange for something?

ALICE. There is nothing to be had on this island.

CURT. Not for my sake, but for his and yours—let me think up something—something. We must make the whole thing

seem laughable when he comes. I'll propose that we have
a drink, and in the meantime I'll think of something. Put
him in good humour; play for him, any old nonsense. Sit
down at the piano and make yourself ready——

ALICE. Look at my hands—are they fit to play with? I
have to wipe glasses and polish brass, sweep floors, and make
fires——

CURT. But you have two servants?

ALICE. So we have to pretend because he is an officer—
but the servants are leaving us all the time, so that often we
have none at all—most of the time, in fact. How am I to
get out of this—this about supper? Oh, if only fire would
break out in this house!

CURT. Don't, Alice, don't!

ALICE. If the sea would rise and take us away!

CURT. No, no, no, I cannot listen to you!

ALICE. What will he say, what will he say— Don't go,
Curt, don't go away from me!

CURT. No, dear Alice— I shall not go.

ALICE. Yes, but when you are gone——

CURT. Has he ever laid hands on you?

ALICE. On me? Oh, no, for he knew that then I should
have left him. One has to preserve some pride.

  From without is heard: "Who goes there?— Friend."

CURT. [*Rising*] Is he coming?

ALICE. [*Frightened*] Yes, that's he.   [*Pause.*

CURT. What in the world are we to do?

ALICE. I don't know, I don't know!

CAPTAIN. [*Enters from the background, cheerful*] There!
Leisure now! Well, has she had time to make her complaints? Is she not unhappy—hey?

CURT. How's the weather outside?

CAPTAIN. Half storm— [*Facetiously; opening one of the doors ajar*] Sir Bluebeard with the maiden in the tower; and outside stands the sentry with drawn sabre to guard the pretty maiden—and then come the brothers, but the sentry is there. Look at him. Hip—hip! That's a fine sentry. Look at him. *Malbrough s'en va-t-en guerre!* Let us dance the sword dance! Curt ought to see it!

CURT. No, let us have "The Entry of the Boyars" instead!

CAPTAIN. Oh, you know that one, do you?— Alice in the kitchen apron, come and play. Come, I tell you!

> [ALICE *goes reluctantly to the piano.*

CAPTAIN. [*Pinching her arm*] Now you have been black-guarding me!

ALICE. I?

> CURT *turns away from them.*
>
> ALICE *plays " The Entry of the Boyars."*
>
> The CAPTAIN *performs some kind of Hungarian dance step behind the writing-table so that his spurs are set jingling. Then he sinks down on the floor without being noticed by* CURT *and* ALICE, *and the latter goes on playing the piece to the end.*

ALICE. [*Without turning around*] Shall we have it again? [*Silence. Turns around and becomes aware of the* CAPTAIN, *who is lying unconscious on the floor in such a way that he is hidden from the public by the writing-table*] Lord Jesus!

> *She stands still, with arms crossed over her breast, and gives vent to a sigh as of gratitude and relief.*

CURT. [*Turns around; hurries over to the* CAPTAIN] What is it? What is it?

ALICE. [*In a high state of tension*] Is he dead?

CURT. I don't know. Come and help me.

ALICE. [*Remains still*] I cannot touch him—is he dead?

CURT. No—he lives.

ALICE *sighs.*

CURT *helps the* CAPTAIN *to his feet and places him in a chair.*

CAPTAIN. What was it? [*Silence*] What was it?

CURT. You fell down.

CAPTAIN. Did anything happen?

CURT. You fell on the floor.   What is the matter with you?

CAPTAIN. With me? Nothing at all I don't know of anything. What are you staring at me for?

CURT. You are ill.

CAPTAIN. What nonsense is that? You go on playing, Alice— Oh, now it's back again!

[*Puts both hands up to his head.*

ALICE. Can't you see that you are ill?

CAPTAIN. Don't shriek! It is only a fainting spell.

CURT. We must call a doctor— I'll use your telephone——

CAPTAIN. I don't want any doctor.

CURT. You must! We have to call him for our own sake —otherwise we shall be held responsible——

CAPTAIN. I'll show him the door if he comes here. I'll shoot him. Oh, now it's there again!

[*Takes hold of his head.*

CURT. [*Goes toward the door on the right*] Now I am going to telephone!   [*Goes out.*

[ALICE *takes off her apron*

CAPTAIN. Will you give me a glass of water?

ALICE. I suppose I have to!   [*Gives him a glass of water.*

CAPTAIN. How amiable!

ALICE. Are you ill?

CAPTAIN. Please pardon me for not being well.

ALICE. Will you take care of yourself then?

CAPTAIN. *You* won't do it, I suppose?

ALICE. No, of that you may be sure!

CAPTAIN. The hour is come for which you have been waiting so long.

ALICE. The hour you believed would never come.

CAPTAIN. Don't be angry with me!

CURT. [*Enters from the right*] Oh, it's too bad——

ALICE. What did he say?

CURT. He rang off without a word.

ALICE. [*To the* CAPTAIN] There is the result of your limitless arrogance!

CAPTAIN. I think I am growing worse— Try to get a doctor from the city.

ALICE. [*Goes to the telegraph instrument*] We shall have to use the telegraph then.

CAPTAIN. [*Rising half-way from the chair; startled*] Do you—know—how to use it?

ALICE. [*Working the key*] Yes, I do.

CAPTAIN. So-o! Well, go on then—But isn't she treacherous! [*To* CURT] Come over here and sit by me. [CURT *sits down beside the* CAPTAIN] Take my hand. I sit here and fall—can you make it out? Down something—such a queer feeling.

CURT. Have you had any attack like this before?

CAPTAIN. Never——

CURT. While you are waiting for an answer from the city, I'll go over to the doctor and have a talk with him. Has he attended you before?

CAPTAIN. He has.

CURT. Then he knows your case. [*Goes toward the left.*

ALICE. There will be an answer shortly. It is very kind of you, Curt. But come back soon.

CURT. As soon as I can.   [*Goes out.*

CAPTAIN. Curt *is* kind! And how he has changed.

ALICE. Yes, and for the better. It is too bad, however, that he must be dragged into our misery just now.

CAPTAIN. But good for us— I wonder just how he stands. Did you notice that he wouldn't speak of his own affairs?

ALICE. I did notice it, but then I don't think anybody asked him.

CAPTAIN. Think, what a life! And ours! I wonder if it is the same for all people?

ALICE. Perhaps, although they don't speak of it as we do.

CAPTAIN. At times I have thought that misery draws misery, and that those who are happy shun the unhappy. That is the reason why we see nothing but misery.

ALICE. Have you known anybody who was happy?

CAPTAIN. Let me see! No— Yes—the Ekmarks.

ALICE. You don't mean it! She had to have an operation last year——

CAPTAIN. That's right. Well, then I don't know—yes, the Von Kraffts.

ALICE. Yes, the whole family lived an idyllic life, well off, respected by everybody, nice children, good marriages— right along until they were fifty. Then that cousin of theirs committed a crime that led to a prison term and all sorts of after-effects. And that was the end of their peace. The family name was dragged in the mud by all the newspapers. The Krafft murder case made it impossible for the family to appear anywhere, after having been so much thought of. The children had to be taken out of school. Oh, heavens!

CAPTAIN. I wonder what my trouble is?

ALICE. What do you think?

CAPTAIN. Heart or head. It is as if the soul wanted to fly off and turn into smoke.

ALICE. Have you any appetite?

CAPTAIN. Yes, how about the supper?

ALICE. [*Crosses the stage, disturbed*] I'll ask Jenny.

CAPTAIN. Why, she's gone!

ALICE. Yes, yes, yes!

CAPTAIN. Ring for Christine so that I can get some fresh water.

ALICE. [*Rings*] I wonder— [*Rings again*] She doesn't hear.

CAPTAIN. Go and look—just think, if she should have left also!

ALICE. [*Goes over to the door on the left and opens it*] What is this? Her trunk is in the hallway—packed.

CAPTAIN. Then she has gone.

ALICE. This is hell!

> *Begins to cry, falls on her knees, and puts her head on a chair, sobbing.*

CAPTAIN. And everything at once! And then Curt had to turn up just in time to get a look into this mess of ours! If there be any further humiliation in store, let it come this moment!

ALICE. Do you know what I suspect? Curt went away and will not come back.

CAPTAIN. I believe it of him.

ALICE. Yes, we are cursed——

CAPTAIN. What are you talking of?

ALICE. Don't you see how everybody shuns us?

CAPTAIN. I don't mind! [*The telegraph receiver clicks*] There is the answer. Hush, I can hear it— Nobody can spare the time. Evasions! The rabble!

ALICE. That's what you get because you have despised your physicians—and failed to pay them.

CAPTAIN. That is not so!

ALICE. Even when you could, you didn't care to pay their bills because you looked down upon their work, just as you have looked down upon mine and everybody else's. They don't want to come. And the telephone is cut off because you

didn't think that good for anything either.   Nothing is good
for anything but your rifles and guns!

CAPTAIN. Don't stand there and talk nonsense——

ALICE. Everything comes back.

CAPTAIN. What sort of superstition is that?   Talk for
old women!

ALICE. You will see!   Do you know that we owe Christine
six months' wages?

CAPTAIN Well, she has stolen that much.

ALICE. But I have also had to borrow money from her.

CAPTAIN. I think you capable of it.

ALICE. What an ingrate you are!   You know I borrowed
that money for the children to get into the city.

CAPTAIN. Curt had a fine way of coming back!   A rascal,
that one, too!   And a coward!   He didn't dare to say he had
had enough, and that he found the doctor's party more pleasant—   He's the same rapscallion as ever!

CURT. [*Enters quickly from the left*] Well, my dear Edgar,
this is how the matter stands—the doctor knows everything
about your heart——

CAPTAIN. My heart?

CURT. You have long been suffering from calcification of
the heart——

CAPTAIN. Stone heart?

CURT. And——

CAPTAIN. Is it serious?

CURT. Well, that is to say——

CAPTAIN. It is serious.

CURT. Yes.

CAPTAIN. Fatal?

CURT. You must be very careful.   First of all: the cigar
must go [*The* CAPTAIN *throws away his cigar*] And next: no
more whiskey!   Then, to bed!

CAPTAIN. [*Scared*] No, I don't want *that!* Not to bed! That's the end! Then you never get up again. I shall sleep on the couch to-night. What more did he say?

CURT. He was very nice about it and will come at once if you call him.

CAPTAIN. Was he nice, the hypocrite? I don't want to see him! I can at least eat?

CURT. Not to-night. And during the next few days nothing but milk.

CAPTAIN. Milk! I cannot take that stuff into my mouth.

CURT. Better learn how!

CAPTAIN. I am too old to learn. [*Puts his hand up to his head*] Oh, there it is again now!

[*He sits perfectly still, staring straight ahead.*

ALICE. [*To* CURT] What did the doctor tell you?

CURT. That he *may* die.

ALICE. Thank God!

CURT. Take care, Alice, take care! And now, go and get a pillow and a blanket and I'll put him here on the couch. Then I'll sit on the chair here all night.

ALICE. And I?

CURT. You go to bed. Your presence seems only to make him worse.

ALICE. Command! I shall obey, for you seem to mean well toward both of us.   [*Goes out to the left.*

CURT. Mark you—toward both of you! And I shall not mix in any partisan squabbles.

CURT *takes the water bottle and goes out to the right. The noise of the wind outside is clearly heard. Then one of the doors is blown open and an old woman of shabby, unprepossessing appearance peeps into the room.*

CAPTAIN. [*Wakes up, rises, and looks around*] So, they have left me, the rascals! [*Catches sight of the old woman and is frightened by her*] Who is it? What do you want?

OLD WOMAN. I just wanted to close the door, sir.

CAPTAIN. Why should you? Why should you?

OLD WOMAN. Because it blew open just as I passed by.

CAPTAIN. Wanted to steal, did you?

OLD WOMAN. Not much here to take away, Christine said.

CAPTAIN. Christine?

OLD WOMAN. Good night, sir, and sleep well!

[*Closes the door and disappears.*
ALICE *comes in from the left with pillows and a blanket.*

CAPTAIN. Who was that at the door? Anybody?

ALICE. Why, it was old Mary from the poorhouse who just went by.

CAPTAIN. Are you sure?

ALICE. Are you afraid?

CAPTAIN. I, afraid? Oh, no!

ALICE. As you don't want to go to bed, you can lie here.

CAPTAIN. [*Goes over to the couch and lies down*] I'll lie here.

[*Tries to take* ALICE'S *hand, but she pulls it away.*
CURT *comes in with the water bottle.*

CAPTAIN. Curt, don't go away from me!

CURT. I am going to stay up with you all night. Alice is going to bed.

CAPTAIN. Good night then, Alice.

ALICE. [*To* CURT] Good night, Curt.

CURT. Good night.

[ALICE *goes out.*

CURT. [*Takes a chair and sits down beside the couch*] Don't you want to take off your boots?

CAPTAIN. No, a warrior should always be armed.

CURT. Are you expecting a battle then?

CAPTAIN. Perhaps! [*Rising up in bed*] Curt, you are the only human being to whom I ever disclosed anything of myself. Listen to me!— If I die to-night—look after my children!

CURT. I will do so.

CAPTAIN. Thank you—I trust in you!

CURT. Can you explain why you trust me?

CAPTAIN. We have not been friends, for friendship is something I don't believe in, and our families were born enemies and have always been at war——

CURT. And yet you trust me?

CAPTAIN. Yes, and I don't know why. [*Silence*] Do you think I am going to die?

CURT. You as well as everybody. There will be no exception made in your case.

CAPTAIN. Are you bitter?

CURT. Yes—are you afraid of death? Of the wheelbarrow and the garden bed?

CAPTAIN. Think, if it were not the end!

CURT. That's what a great many think!

CAPTAIN. And then?

CURT. Nothing but surprises, I suppose.

CAPTAIN. But nothing at all is known with certainty?

CURT. No, that's just it! That is why you must be prepared for everything.

CAPTAIN. You are not childish enough to believe in a hell?

CURT. Do you not believe in it—you, who are right in it?

CAPTAIN. That is metaphorical only.

CURT. The realism with which you have described yours seems to preclude all thought of metaphors, poetical or otherwise.   [*Silence.*

CAPTAIN. If you only knew what pangs I suffer!

CURT. Of the body?

CAPTAIN. No, not of the body.

CURT. Then it must be of the spirit, for no other alternative exists.   [*Pause.*

CAPTAIN. [*Rising up in bed*] I don't want to die!

CURT. Not long ago you wished for annihilation.

CAPTAIN. Yes, if it be painless.

CURT. Apparently it is not!

CAPTAIN. Is this annihilation then?

CURT. The beginning of it.

CAPTAIN. Good night.

CURT. Good night.

Curtain.

The same setting, but now the lamp is at the point of going out. Through the windows and the glass panes of the doors a gray morning is visible. The sea is stirring. The sentry is on the battery as before.

The CAPTAIN *is lying on the couch, asleep.* CURT *sits on a chair beside him, looking pale and wearied from his watch.*

ALICE. [*In from the left*] Is he asleep?

CURT. Yes, since the time when the sun should have risen.

ALICE. What kind of night did he have?

CURT. He slept now and then, but he talked a good deal.

ALICE. Of what?

CURT. He argued about religion like a schoolboy, but with a pretension of having solved all the world riddles. Finally, toward morning, he invented the immortality of the soul.

ALICE. For his own glory.

CURT. Exactly! He is actually the most conceited person I have ever met. "I am; consequently God must be."

ALICE. You have become aware of it? Look at those boots. With those he would have trampled the earth flat, had he been allowed to do so. With those he has trampled down other people's fields and gardens. With those he has trampled on some people's toes and other people's heads— Man-eater, you have got your bullet at last!

CURT. He would be comical were he not so tragical; and there are traces of greatness in all his narrow-mindedness— Have you not a single good word to say about him?

ALICE. [*Sitting down*] Yes, if he only does not hear it; for if he hears a single word of praise he develops megalomania on the spot.

183

CURT. He can hear nothing now, for he has had a dose of morphine.

ALICE. Born in a poor home, with many brothers and sisters, Edgar very early had to support the family by giving lessons, as the father was a ne'er-do-well if nothing worse. It must be hard for a young man to give up all the pleasures of youth in order to slave for a bunch of thankless children whom he has not brought into the world. I was a little girl when I saw him, as a young man, going without an overcoat in the winter while the mercury stood at fifteen below zero—his little sisters wore kersey coats—it was fine, and I admired him, but his ugliness repelled me. Is he not unusually ugly?

CURT. Yes, and his ugliness has a touch of the monstrous at times. Whenever we fell out, I noticed it particularly. And when, at such times, he went away, his image assumed enormous forms and proportions, and he literally haunted me.

ALICE. Think of me then! However, his earlier years as an officer were undoubtedly a martyrdom. But now and then he was helped by rich people. This he will never admit, and whatever has come to him in that way he has accepted as a due tribute, without giving thanks for it.

CURT. We were to speak well of him.

ALICE. Yes—after he is dead. But then I recall nothing more.

CURT. Have you found him cruel?

ALICE. Yes—and yet he can show himself both kind and susceptible to sentiment. As an enemy he is simply horrible.

CURT. Why did he not get the rank of major?

ALICE. Oh, you ought to understand that! They didn't want to raise a man above themselves who had already proved himself a tyrant as an inferior. But you must never let on that you know this. He says himself that he did not want promotion— Did he speak of the children?

CURT. Yes, he was longing for Judith.

ALICE. I thought so— Oh! Do you know what Judith is? His own image, whom he has trained for use against me. Think only, that my own daughter—has raised her hand against me!

CURT. That is too much!

ALICE. Hush! He is moving— Think if he overheard us! He is full of trickery also.

CURT. He is actually waking up.

ALICE. Does he not look like an ogre? I am afraid of him!
[*Silence.*

CAPTAIN. [*Stirs, wakes up, rises in bed, and looks around*] It is morning—at last!

CURT. How are you feeling?

CAPTAIN. Not so very bad.

CURT. Do you want a doctor?

CAPTAIN. No—I want to see Judith—my child!

CURT. Would it not be wise to set your house in order before—or if something should happen?

CAPTAIN. What do you mean? What could happen?

CURT. What may happen to all of us.

CAPTAIN. Oh, nonsense! Don't you believe that I die so easily! And don't rejoice prematurely, Alice!

CURT. Think of your children. Make your will so that your wife at least may keep the household goods.

CAPTAIN. Is she going to inherit from me while I am still alive?

CURT. No, but if something happens she ought not to be turned into the street. One who has dusted and polished and looked after these things for twenty-five years should have some right to remain in possession of them. May I send word to the regimental lawyer?

CAPTAIN. No!

CURT. You are a cruel man—more cruel than I thought you!

CAPTAIN. Now it is back again!

[*Falls back on the bed unconscious.*

ALICE. [*Goes toward the right*] There are some people in the kitchen— I have to go down there.

CURT. Yes, go. Here is not much to be done.

[ALICE *goes out.*

CAPTAIN. [*Recovers*] Well, Curt, what are you going to do about your quarantine?

CURT. Oh, that will be all right.

CAPTAIN. No; I am in command on this island, so you will have to deal with me—don't forget that!

CURT. Have you ever seen a quarantine station?

CAPTAIN. Have I? Before you were born. And I'll give you a piece of advice: don't place your disinfection plant too close to the shore.

CURT. I was thinking that the nearer I could get to the water the better——

CAPTAIN. That shows how much you know of your business. Water, don't you see, is the element of the bacilli, their life element?

CURT. But the salt water of the sea is needed to wash away all the impurity.

CAPTAIN. Idiot! Well, now, when you get a house for yourself I suppose you'll bring home your children?

CURT. Do you think they will let themselves be brought?

CAPTAIN. Of course, if you have got any backbone! It would make a good impression on the people if you fulfilled your duties in that respect also——

CURT. I have always fulfilled my duties in that respect.

CAPTAIN. [*Raising his voice*] —in the one respect where you have proved yourself most remiss——

CURT. Have I not told you——

CAPTAIN. [*Paying no attention*] —for one does not desert one's children like that——

CURT. Go right on!

CAPTAIN. As your relative—a relative older than yourself —I feel entitled to tell you the truth, even if it should prove bitter—and you should not take it badly——

CURT. Are you hungry?

CAPTAIN. Yes, I am.

CURT. Do you want something light?

CAPTAIN. No, something solid.

CURT. Then you would be done for.

CAPTAIN. Is it not enough to be sick, but one must starve also?

CURT. That's how the land lies.

CAPTAIN. And neither drink nor smoke? Then life is not worth much!

CURT. Death demands sacrifices, or it comes at once.

ALICE. [*Enters with several bunches of flowers and some telegrams and letters*] These are for you.

[*Throws the flowers on the writing-table.*

CAPTAIN. [*Flattered*] For me! Will you please let me look?

ALICE. Oh, they are only from the non-commissioned officers, the bandmen, and the gunners.

CAPTAIN. You are jealous.

ALICE. Oh, no. If it were laurel wreaths, that would be another matter—but those you can never get.

CAPTAIN. Hm!— Here's a telegram from the Colonel— read it, Curt. The Colonel is a gentleman after all—though he is something of an idiot. And this is from—what does it say? It is from Judith! Please telegraph her to come with the next boat. And here—yes, one is not quite without friends after all, and it is fine to see them take thought of a sick man, who is also a man of deserts above his rank, and a man free of fear or blemish

ALICE. I don't quite understand—are they congratulating you because you are sick?

CAPTAIN. Hyena!

ALICE. Yes, we had a doctor here on the island who was so hated that when he left they gave a banquet—after him, and not for him!

CAPTAIN. Put the flowers in water—I am not easily caught, and all people are a lot of rabble, but, by heavens, these simple tributes are genuine—they cannot be anything but genuine!

ALICE. Fool!

CURT. [*Reading the telegram*] Judith says she cannot come because the steamer is held back by the storm.

CAPTAIN. Is that all?

CURT. No-o—there is a postscript.

CAPTAIN. Out with it!

CURT. Well, she asks her father not to drink so much.

CAPTAIN. Impudence! That's like children! That's my only beloved daughter—my Judith—my idol!

ALICE. And your image!

CAPTAIN. Such is life. Such are its best joys— Hell!

ALICE. Now you get the harvest of your sowing. You have set her against her own mother and now she turns against the father. Tell me, then, that there is no God!

CAPTAIN. [*To* CURT] What does the Colonel say?

CURT. He grants leave of absence without any comment.

CAPTAIN. Leave of absence? I have not asked for it.

ALICE. No, but I have asked for it.

CAPTAIN. I don't accept it.

ALICE. Order has already been issued.

CAPTAIN. That's none of my concern!

ALICE. Do you see, Curt, that for this man exist no laws,

no constitutions, no prescribed human order? He stands
above everything and everybody. The universe is created
for his private use. The sun and the moon pursue their
courses in order to spread his glory among the stars. Such
is this man: this insignificant captain, who could not even
reach the rank of major, and at whose strutting everybody
laughs, while he thinks himself feared; this poor wretch who
is afraid in the dark and believes in barometers: and all this
in conjunction with and having for its climax—a barrowful
of manure that is not even prime quality!

CAPTAIN. [*Fanning himself with a bunch of flowers, con-
ceitedly, without listening to* ALICE] Have you asked Curt to
breakfast?

ALICE. No.

CAPTAIN. Get us, then, at once two nice tenderloin steaks.

ALICE. Two?

CAPTAIN. I am going to have one myself.

ALICE. But we are three here.

CAPTAIN. Oh, you want one also? Well, make it three
then.

ALICE. Where am I to get them? Last night you asked
Curt to supper, and there was not a crust of bread in the
house. Curt has been awake all night without anything to
eat, and he has had no coffee because there is none in the
house and the credit is gone.

CAPTAIN. She is angry at me for not dying yesterday.

ALICE. No, for not dying twenty-five years ago—for not
dying before you were born!

CAPTAIN. [*To* CURT] Listen to her! That's what happens
when you institute a marriage, my dear Curt. And it is perfectly clear that it was not instituted in heaven.

[ALICE *and* CURT *look at each other meaningly.*

CAPTAIN. [*Rises and goes toward the door*] However, say

what you will, now I am going on duty. [*Puts on an old-fashioned helmet with a brush crest, girds on the sabre, and shoulders his cloak*] If anybody calls for me, I am at the battery. [ALICE *and* CURT *try vainly to hold him back*] Stand aside!

[*Goes out.*

ALICE. Yes, go! You always go, always show your back, whenever the fight becomes too much for you. And then you let your wife cover the retreat—you hero of the bottle, you arch-braggart, you arch-liar! Fie on you!

CURT. This is bottomless!

ALICE. And you don't know everything yet.

CURT. Is there anything more——

ALICE. But I am ashamed——

CURT. Where is he going now? And where does he get the strength?

ALICE. Yes, you may well ask! Now he goes down to the non-commissioned officers and thanks them for the flowers—and then he eats and drinks with them. And then he speaks ill of all the other officers— If you only knew how many times he has been threatened with discharge! Nothing but sympathy for his family has saved him. And this he takes for fear of his superiority. And he hates and maligns the very women—wives of other officers—who have been pleading our cause.

CURT. I have to confess that I applied for this position in order to find peace by the sea—and of your circumstances I knew nothing at all.

ALICE. Poor Curt! And how will you get something to eat?

CURT. Oh, I can go over to the doctor's—but you? Will you not permit me to arrange this for you?

ALICE. If only he does not learn of it, for then he would kill me.

CURT. [*Looking out through the window*] Look, he stands right in the wind out there on the rampart.

ALICE. He is to be pitied—for being what he is!

CURT. Both of you are to be pitied! But what can be done?

ALICE. I don't know— The mail brought a batch of unpaid bills also, and those he did not see.

CURT. It may be fortunate to escape seeing things at times.

ALICE. [*At the window*] He has unbuttoned his cloak and lets the wind strike his chest. Now he wants to die!

CURT. That is not what he wants, I think, for a while ago, when he felt his life slipping away, he grabbed hold of mine and began to stir in my affairs as if he wanted to crawl into me and live my life.

ALICE. That is just his vampire nature—to interfere with other people's destinies, to suck interest out of other existences, to regulate and arrange the doings of others, since he can find no interest whatever in his own life. And remember, Curt, don't ever admit him into your family life, don't ever make him acquainted with your friends, for he will take them away from you and make them his own. He is a perfect magician in this respect. Were he to meet your children, you would soon find them intimate with *him,* and he would be advising them and educating them to suit himself—but principally in opposition to *your* wishes.

CURT. Alice, was it not he who took my children away from me at the time of the divorce?

ALICE. Since it is all over now—yes, it was he.

CURT. I have suspected it, but never had any certainty. It was he!

ALICE. When you placed your full trust in my husband and sent him to make peace between yourself and your wife, he made love to her instead, and taught her the trick that gave her the children.

CURT. Oh, God! God in heaven!

ALICE. There you have another side of him.　　[*Silence.*

CURT. Do you know, last night—when he thought himself dying—then—he made me promise that 1 should look after his children!

ALICE. But you don't want to revenge yourself on my children?

CURT. Yes—by keeping my promise. I shall look after your children.

ALICE. You could take no worse revenge, for there is nothing he hates so much as generosity.

CURT. Then I may consider myself revenged—without any revenge.

ALICE. I love revenge as a form of justice, and I am yearning to see evil get its punishment.

CURT. You still remain at that point?

ALICE. There I shall always remain, and the day I forgave or loved an enemy I should be a hypocrite.

CURT. It may be a duty not to say everything, Alice, not to see everything. It is called forbearance, and all of us need it.

ALICE. Not I! My life lies clear and open, and I have always played my cards straight.

CURT. That is saying a good deal.

ALICE. No, it is not saying enough. Because what I have suffered innocently for the sake of this man, whom I never loved——

CURT. Why did you marry?

ALICE. Who can tell? Because he took me, seduced me! I don't know. And then I was longing to get up on the heights——

CURT. And deserted your art?

ALICE. Which was despised! But you know, he cheated me! He held out hopes of a pleasant life, a handsome home —and there was nothing but debts; no gold except on the uniform—and even that was not real gold. He cheated me!

CURT. Wait a moment! When a young man falls in love, he sees the future in a hopeful light: that his hopes are not always realized, one must pardon. I have the same kind of deceit on my own conscience without thinking myself dishonest— What is it you see on the rampart?

ALICE. I want to see if he has fallen down.

CURT. Has he?

ALICE. No—worse luck! He is cheating me all the time.

CURT. Then I shall call on the doctor and the lawyer.

ALICE. [*Sitting down at the window*] Yes, dear Curt, go. I shall sit here and wait. And I have learned how to wait!

Curtain.

Same setting in full daylight. The sentry is pacing back and forth on the battery as before.

    ALICE *sits in the right-hand easy-chair. Her hair is now gray.*

CURT. [*Enters from the left after having knocked*] Good day, Alice.

ALICE. Good day, Curt. Sit down.

CURT. [*Sits down in the left-hand easy-chair*] The steamer is just coming in.

ALICE. Then I know what's in store, for he is on board.

CURT. Yes, he is, for I caught the glitter of his helmet— What has he been doing in the city?

ALICE. Oh, I can figure it out. He dressed for parade, which means that he saw the Colonel, and he put on white gloves, which means that he made some calls.

CURT. Did you notice his quiet manner yesterday? Since he has quit drinking and become temperate, he is another man: calm, reserved, considerate——

ALICE. I know it, and if that man had always kept sober he would have been a menace to humanity. It is perhaps fortunate for the rest of mankind that he made himself ridiculous and harmless through his whiskey.

CURT. The spirit in the bottle has chastised him— But have you noticed since death put its mark on him that he has developed a dignity which elevates? And is it not possible that with this new idea of immortality may have come a new outlook upon life?

ALICE. You are deceiving yourself. He is conjuring up something evil. And don't you believe what he says, for he

194

lies with premeditation, and he knows the art of intriguing as no one else——

CURT. [*Watching* ALICE] Why, Alice, what does this mean? Your hair has turned gray in these two nights!

ALICE. No, my friend, it has long been gray, and I have simply neglected to darken it since my husband is as good as dead. Twenty-five years in prison—do you know that this place served as a prison in the old days?

CURT. Prison—well, the walls show it.

ALICE. And my complexion! Even the children took on prison color in here.

CURT. I find it hard to imagine children prattling within these walls.

ALICE. There was not much prattling done either. And those two that died perished merely from lack of light.

CURT. What do you think is coming next?

ALICE. The decisive blow at us two. I caught a familiar glimmer in his eye when you read out that telegram from Judith. It ought, of course, to have been directed against her, but she, you know, is inviolate, and so his hatred sought you.

CURT. What are his intentions in regard to me, do you think?

ALICE. Hard to tell, but he possesses a marvellous skill in nosing out other people's secrets—and did you notice how, all day yesterday, he seemed to be living in your quarantine; how he drank a life-interest out of your existence; how he ate your children alive? A cannibal, I tell you—for I know him. His own life is going, or has gone——

CURT. I also have that impression of his being already on the other side. His face seems to phosphoresce, as if he were in a state of decay—and his eyes flash like will-o'-the-wisps over graves or morasses— Here he comes! Tell him you thought it possible he might be jealous.

ALICE. No, he is too self-conceited. "Show me the man of whom I need to be jealous!" Those are his own words.

CURT. So much the better, for even his faults carry with them a certain merit— Shall I get up and meet him anyhow?

ALICE. No, be impolite, or he will think you false. And if he begins to lie, pretend to believe him. I know perfectly how to translate his lies, and get always at the truth with the help of my dictionary. I foresee something dreadful—but, Curt, don't lose your self-control! My own advantage in our long struggle has been that I was always sober, and for that reason in full control of myself. He was always tripped by his whiskey— Now we shall see!

CAPTAIN. [*In from the left in full uniform, with helmet, cloak, and white gloves. Calm, dignified, but pale and hollow-eyed. Moves forward with a tottering step and sinks down, his helmet and cloak still on, in a chair at the right of the stage, far from* CURT *and* ALICE] Good day. Pardon me for sitting down like this, but I feel a little tired.

ALICE *and* CURT. Good day. Welcome home.

ALICE. How are you feeling?

CAPTAIN. Splendid! Only a little tired——

ALICE. What news from the city?

CAPTAIN. Oh, a little of everything. I saw the doctor, among other things, and he said it was nothing at all—that I might live twenty years, if I took care of myself.

ALICE. [*To* CURT] Now he is lying. [*To the* CAPTAIN] Why, that's fine, my dear.

CAPTAIN. So much for that.

   Silence, during which the CAPTAIN *is looking at* ALICE
      and CURT *as if expecting them to speak.*

ALICE. [*To* CURT] Don't say a word, but let him begin— then he will show his cards.

CAPTAIN. [*To* ALICE] Did you say anything?

ALICE. No, not a word.

CAPTAIN. [*Dragging on the words*] Well, Curt!

ALICE. [*To CURT*] There—now he is coming out.

CAPTAIN. Well, I went to the city, as you know. [CURT *nods assent*] Mm-mm, I picked up acquaintances—and among others—a young cadet [*dragging*] in the artillery. [*Pause, during which* CURT *shows some agitation*] As—we are in need of cadets right here, I arranged with the Colonel to let him come here. This ought to please you, especially when I inform you that—he is—your own son!

ALICE. [*To CURT*] The vampire—don't you see?

CURT. Under ordinary circumstances that ought to please a father, but in my case it will merely be painful.

CAPTAIN. I don't see why it should!

CURT. You don't need to—it is enough that I don't want it.

CAPTAIN. Oh, you think so? Well, then, you ought to know that the young man has been ordered to report here, and that from now on he has to obey me.

CURT. Then I shall force him to seek transfer to another regiment.

CAPTAIN. You cannot do it, as you have no rights over your son.

CURT. No?

CAPTAIN. No, for the court gave those rights to the mother.

CURT. Then I shall communicate with the mother.

CAPTAIN. You don't need to.

CURT. Don't need to?

CAPTAIN. No, for I have already done so. Yah!

[CURT *rises but sinks back again.*

ALICE. [*To CURT*] Now he must die!

CURT. Why, he *is* a cannibal!

CAPTAIN. So much for that! [*Straight to* ALICE *and* CURT] Did you say anything?

ALICE. No—have you grown hard of hearing?

CAPTAIN. Yes, a little—but if you come nearer to me I can tell you something between ourselves.

ALICE. That is not necessary—and a witness is sometimes good to have for both parties.

CAPTAIN. You are right; witnesses are sometimes good to have! But, first of all, did you get that will?

ALICE. [*Hands him a document*] The regimental lawyer drew it up himself.

CAPTAIN. In your favor—good! [*Reads the document and then tears it carefully into strips which he throws on the floor*] So much for that! Yah!

ALICE. [*To* CURT] Did you ever see such a man?

CURT. That is no man!

CAPTAIN. Well, Alice, this was what I wanted to say——

ALICE. [*Alarmed*] Go on, please.

CAPTAIN. [*Calmly as before*] On account of your long cherished desire to quit this miserable existence in an unhappy marriage; on account of the lack of feeling with which you have treated your husband and children, and on account of the carelessness you have shown in the handling of our domestic economy, I have, during this trip to the city, filed an application for divorce in the City Court.

ALICE. Oh—and your grounds?

CAPTAIN. [*Calmly as before*] Besides the grounds already mentioned, I have others of a purely personal nature. As it has been found that I may live another twenty years, I am contemplating a change from this unhappy marital union to one that suits me better, and I mean to join my fate to that of some woman capable of devotion to her husband, and who also may bring into the home not only youth, but—let us say—a little beauty!

ALICE. [*Takes the wedding-ring from her finger and throws it at the* CAPTAIN] You are welcome!

CAPTAIN. [*Picks up the ring and puts it in his vest pocket*] She throws away the ring. The witness will please take notice.

ALICE. [*Rises in great agitation*] And you intend to turn me out in order to put another woman into my home?

CAPTAIN. Yah!

ALICE. Well, then, we'll speak plain language! Cousin Curt, that man is guilty of an attempt to murder his wife.

CURT. An attempt to murder?

ALICE. Yes, he pushed me into the water.

CAPTAIN. Without witnesses!

ALICE. He lies again—Judith saw it!

CAPTAIN. Well, what of it?

ALICE. She can testify to it.

CAPTAIN. No, she cannot, for she says that she didn't see anything.

ALICE. You have taught the child to lie!

CAPTAIN. I didn't need to, for you had taught her already.

ALICE. You have met Judith?

CAPTAIN. Yah!

ALICE. Oh, God! Oh, God!

CAPTAIN. The fortress has surrendered. The enemy will be permitted to depart in safety on ten minutes' notice. [*Places his watch on the table*] Ten minutes—watch on the table!   [*Stops and puts one hand up to his heart.*

ALICE. [*Goes over to the* CAPTAIN *and takes his arm*] What is it?

CAPTAIN. I don't know.

ALICE. Do you want anything—a drink?

CAPTAIN. Whiskey? No, I don't want to die— You! [*Straightening himself up*] Don't touch me! Ten minutes, or the garrison will be massacred. [*Pulls the sabre partly from the scabbard*] Ten minutes!

[*Goes out through the background.*

CURT. What kind of man is this?

ALICE. He is a demon, and no man!

CURT. What does he want with my son?

ALICE. He wants him as hostage in order to be your master—he wants to isolate you from the authorities of the island— Do you know that the people around here have named this island "Little Hell"?

CURT. I didn't know that— Alice, you are the first woman who ever inspired me with compassion—all others have seemed to me to deserve their fate.

ALICE. Don't desert me now! Don't leave me, for he will beat me—he has been doing so all these twenty-five years—in the presence of the children—and he has pushed me into the water——

CURT. Having heard this, I place myself absolutely against him. I came here without an angry thought, without memory of his former slanders and attempts to humiliate me. I forgave him even when you told me that he was the man who had parted me from my children—for he was ill and dying—but now, when he wants to steal my son, he must die—he or I!

ALICE. Good! No surrender of the fortress! But blow it up instead, with him in it, even if we have to keep him company! I am in charge of the powder!

CURT. There was no malice in me when I came here, and I wanted to run away when I felt myself infected with your hatred, but now I am moved by an irresistible impulse to hate this man, as I hate everything that is evil. What can be done?

ALICE. I have learned the tactics from him. Drum up his enemies and seek allies.

CURT. Just think—that he should get hold of my wife! Why didn't those two meet a life-time ago? Then there would have been a battle-royal that had set the earth quaking.

ALICE. But now these souls have spied each other—and yet they must part. I guess what is his most vulnerable spot— I have long suspected it——

CURT. Who is his most faithful enemy on the island?

ALICE. The Quartermaster.

CURT. Is he an honest man?

ALICE. He is. And he knows what I—I know too—he knows what the Sergeant-Major and the Captain have been up to.

CURT. What they have been up to? You don't mean——

ALICE. Defalcations!

CURT. This is terrible! No, I don't want to have any finger in that mess!

ALICE. Ha-ha! You cannot hit an enemy.

CURT. Formerly I could, but I can do so no longer.

ALICE. Why?

CURT. Because I have discovered—that justice is done anyhow.

ALICE. And you could wait for that? Then your son would already have been taken away from you. Look at my gray hairs—just feel how thick it still is, for that matter— He intends to marry again, and then I shall be free—to do the same— I am free! And in ten minutes he will be under arrest down below, right under us—[stamps her foot on the floor] right under us—and I shall dance above his head—I shall dance "The Entry of the Boyars"—[makes a few steps with her arms akimbo] ha-ha-ha-ha! And I shall play on the piano so that he can hear it. [Hammering on the piano] Oh, the tower is opening its gates, and the sentry with the drawn sabre will no longer be guarding me, but him—Malrough *s'en va-t-en guerre!* Him, him, him, the sentry is going to guard!

CURT. [*Has been watching her with an intoxicated look in his eyes*] Alice, are you, too, a devil?

ALICE. [*Jumps up on a chair and pulls down the wreaths*] These we will take along when we depart—the laurels of triumph! And fluttering ribbons! A little dusty, but eternally green—like my youth— I am not old, Curt?

CURT. [*With shining eyes*] You are a devil!

ALICE. In "Little Hell"— Listen! Now I shall fix my hair —[*loosens her hair*], dress in two minutes—go to the Quartermaster in two minutes—and then, up in the air with the fortress!

CURT. [*As before*] You are a devil!

ALICE. That's what you always used to say when we were children. Do you remember when we were small and became engaged to each other? Ha-ha! You were bashful, of course——

CURT. [*Seriously*] Alice!

ALICE. Yes, you were! And it was becoming to you. Do you know there are gross women who like modest men? And there are said to be modest men who like gross women— You liked me a little bit, didn't you?

CURT. I don't know where I am!

ALICE. With an actress whose manners are free, but who is an excellent lady otherwise. Yes! But now I am free, free, free! Turn away and I'll change my waist!

> *She opens her waist.* CURT *rushes up to her, grabs her in his arms, lifts her high up, and bites her throat so that she cries out. Then he drops her on the couch and runs out to the left.*

> *Curtain and intermission.*

*Same stage setting in early evening light. The sentry on the bat-
tery is still visible through the windows in the background.
The laurel wreaths are hung over the arms of an easy-
chair. The hanging lamp is lit. Faint music.*

> *The* CAPTAIN, *pale and hollow-eyed, his hair showing
> touches of gray, dressed in a worn undress uniform,
> with riding-boots, sits at the writing-table and plays
> solitaire. He wears his spectacles. The entr'acte
> music continues after the curtain has been raised and
> until another person enters.*

> *The* CAPTAIN *plays away at his solitaire, but with a
> sudden start now and then, when he looks up and lis-
> tens with evident alarm.*

> *He does not seem able to make the solitaire come out, so
> he becomes impatient and gathers up the cards. Then
> he goes to the left-hand window, opens it, and throws
> out the cards. The window (of the French type) re-
> mains open, rattling on its hinges.*

> *He goes over to the buffet, but is frightened by the noise
> made by the window, so that he turns around to see
> what it is. Takes out three dark-coloured square whis-
> key bottles, examines them carefully—and throws them
> out of the window. Takes out some boxes of cigars,
> smells at one, and throws them out of the window.*

> *Next he takes off his spectacles, cleans them carefully,
> and tries how far he can see with them. Then he
> throws them out of the window, stumbles against the
> furniture as if he could not see, and lights six candles
> in a candelabrum on the chiffonier. Catches sight of
> the laurel wreaths, picks them up, and goes toward the
> window, but turns back. Folds the wreaths carefully*

in the piano cover, fastens the corners together with pins taken from the writing-table, and puts the bundle on a chair. Goes to the piano, strikes the keyboard with his fists, locks the piano, and throws the key out through the window. Then he lights the candles on the piano. Goes to the what-not, takes his wife's picture from it, looks at this and tears it to pieces, dropping the pieces on the floor. The window rattles on its hinges, and again he becomes frightened.

Then, after having calmed himself, he takes the pictures of his son and daughter, kisses them in an off-hand way, and puts them into his pocket. All the rest of the pictures he sweeps down with his elbow and pokes together into a heap with his foot.

Then he sits down at the writing-table, tired out, and puts a hand up to his heart. Lights the candle on the table and sighs: stares in front of himself as if confronted with unpleasant visions. Rises and goes over to the chiffonier, opens the lid, takes out a bundle of letters tied together with a blue silk ribbon, and throws the bundle into the fireplace of the glazed brick oven. Closes the chiffonier. The telegraph receiver sounds a single click. The CAPTAIN *shrinks together in deadly fear and stands fixed to the spot, listening. But hearing nothing more from the instrument, he turns to listen in the direction of the door on the left. Goes over and opens it, takes a step inside the doorway, and returns, carrying on his arm a cat whose back he strokes. Then he goes out to the right. Now the music ceases.*

ALICE *enters from the background, dressed in a walking suit, with gloves and hat on; her hair is black; she looks around with surprise at the many lighted candles.*

CURT *enters from the left, nervous.*

ALICE. It looks like Christmas Eve here.

CURT. Well?

ALICE. [*Holds out her hand for him to kiss*] Thank me! [CURT *kisses her hand unwillingly*] Six witnesses, and four of them solid as rock. The report has been made, and the answer will come here by telegraph—right here, into the heart of the fortress.

CURT. So!

ALICE. You should say "thanks" instead of "so."

CURT. Why has he lit so many candles?

ALICE. Because he is afraid of the dark, of course. Look at the telegraph key—does it not look like the handle of a coffee mill? I grind, I grind, and the beans crack as when you pull teeth——

CURT. What has he been doing in the room here?

ALICE. It looks as if he intended to move. Down below, that's where you are going to move!

CURT. Don't, Alice—I think it's distressing! He was the friend of my youth, and he showed me kindness many times when I was in difficulty— He should be pitied!

ALICE. And how about me, who have done nothing wrong, and who have had to sacrifice my career to that monster?

CURT. How about that career? Was it so very brilliant?

ALICE. [*Enraged*] What are you saying? Do you know who I am, what I have been?

CURT. Now, now!

ALICE. Are you beginning already?

CURT. Already?

> ALICE *throws her arms around* CURT's *neck and kisses him.*
>
> CURT *takes her by the arms and bites her neck so that she screams.*

ALICE. You bite me!

CURT. [*Beyond himself*] Yes, I want to bite your throat and suck your blood like a lynx. You have aroused the wild beast in me—that beast which I have tried for years to kill by privations and self-inflicted tortures. I came here believing myself a little better than you two, and now I am the vilest of all. Since I first saw you—in all your odious nakedness—and since my vision became warped by passion, I have known the full strength of evil. What is ugly becomes beautiful; what is good becomes ugly and mean— Come here and I'll choke you—with a kiss!   [*He locks her in his arms.*

ALICE. [*Holds up her left hand*] Behold the mark of the shackles that you have broken. I was a slave, and you set me free.

CURT. But I am going to bind you——

ALICE. You?

CURT. I!

ALICE. For a moment I thought you were——

CURT. Pious?

ALICE. Yes, you prated about the fall of man——

CURT. Did I?

ALICE. And I thought you had come here to preach——

CURT. You thought so? In an hour we shall be in the city, and then you shall see what I am——

ALICE. Then we will go to the theatre to-night, just to show ourselves. The shame will be his if I run away, don't you see!

CURT. I begin to understand that prison is not enough——

ALICE. No, it is not—there must be shame also.

CURT. A strange world! You commit a shameful act, and the shame falls on him.

ALICE. Well, if the world be so stupid——

CURT. It is as if these prison walls had absorbed all the corruption of the criminals, and it gets into you if you merely breathe this air. You were thinking of the theatre and the supper, I suppose. I was thinking of my son.

ALICE. [*Strikes him on the mouth with her glove*] Fogey!

[CURT *lifts his hand as if to strike her.*

ALICE. [*Drawing back*] Tout beau!

CURT. Forgive me!

ALICE. Yes—on your knees! [CURT *kneels down*] Down on your face! [CURT *touches the ground with his forehead*] Kiss my foot! [CURT *kisses her foot*] And don't you ever do it again! Get up!

CURT. [*Rising*] Where have I landed? Where am I?

ALICE. Oh, you know!

CURT. [*Looking around with horror*] I believe almost——

CAPTAIN. [*Enters from the right, looking wretched, leaning on a cane*] Curt, may I have a talk with you—alone?

ALICE. Is it about that departure in safety?

CAPTAIN. [*Sits down at the sewing-table*] Curt, will you kindly sit down here by me a little while? And, Alice, will you please grant me a moment—of peace!

ALICE. What is up now? New signals! [*To* CURT] Please be seated. [CURT *sits down reluctantly*] And listen to the words of age and wisdom— And if a telegram should come—tip me off!   [*Goes out to the left.*

CAPTAIN. [*With dignity, after a pause*] Can you explain a fate like mine, like ours?

CURT. No more than I can explain my own!

CAPTAIN. What can be the meaning of this jumble?

CURT. In my better moments I have believed that just this was the meaning—that we should not be able to catch a meaning, and yet submit——

CAPTAIN. Submit? Without a fixed point outside myself I cannot submit.

CURT. Quite right, but as a mathematician you should be able to seek that unknown point when several known ones are given——

CAPTAIN. I have sought it, and—I have not found it!

CURT. Then you have made some mistake in your calculations—do it all over again!

CAPTAIN. I should do it over again? Tell me, where did you get your resignation?

CURT. I have none left. Don't overestimate me.

CAPTAIN. As you may have noticed, my understanding of the art of living has been—elimination! That means: wipe out and pass on! Very early in life I made myself a bag into which I chucked my humiliations, and when it was full I dropped it into the sea. I don't think any man ever suffered so many humiliations as I have. But when I wiped them out and passed on they ceased to exist.

CURT. I have noticed that you have wrought both your life and your environment out of your poetical imagination.

CAPTAIN. How could I have lived otherwise? How could I have endured?   [Puts his hand over his heart.

CURT. How are you doing?

CAPTAIN. Poorly. [Pause] Then comes a moment when the faculty for what you call poetical imagination gives out. And then reality leaps forth in all its nakedness— It is frightful! [He is now speaking in a voice of lachrymose senility, and with his lower jaw drooping] Look here, my dear friend— [controls himself and speaks in his usual voice] forgive me!— When I was in the city and consulted the doctor [now the tearful voice returns] he said that I was played out—[in his usual voice] and that I couldn't live much longer.

CURT. Was that what he said?

CAPTAIN. [With tearful voice] That's what he said!

CURT. So it was not true?

CAPTAIN. What? Oh—no, that was not true.   [*Pause.*

CURT. Was the rest of it not true either?

CAPTAIN. What do you mean?

CURT. That my son was ordered to report here as cadet?

CAPTAIN. I never heard of it.

CURT. Do you know—your ability to wipe out your own misdeeds is miraculous!

CAPTAIN. I don't understand what you are talking of.

CURT. Then you have come to the end!

CAPTAIN. Well, there is not much left!

CURT. Tell me, perhaps you never applied for that divorce which would bring your wife into disgrace?

CAPTAIN. Divorce? No, I have not heard of it.

CURT. [*Rising*] Will you admit, then, that you have been lying?

CAPTAIN. You employ such strong words, my friend. All of us need forbearance.

CURT. Oh, you have come to see that?

CAPTAIN. [*Firmly, with clear voice*] Yes, I have come to see that— And for this reason, Curt, please forgive me! Forgive everything!

CURT. That was a manly word! But I have nothing to forgive you. And I am not the man you believe me to be. No longer now! Least of all one worthy of receiving your confessions!

CAPTAIN. [*With clear voice*] Life seemed so peculiar—so contrary, so malignant—ever since my childhood—and people seemed so bad that I grew bad also——

CURT. [*On his feet, perturbed, and glancing at the telegraph instrument*] Is it possible to close off an instrument like that?

CAPTAIN. Hardly.

CURT. [*With increasing alarm*] Who is Sergeant-Major Östberg?

CAPTAIN. An honest fellow, but something of a busybody, I should say.

CURT. And who is the Quartermaster?

CAPTAIN. He is my enemy, of course, but I have nothing bad to say of him.

CURT. [*Looking out through the window, where a lantern is seen moving to and fro*] What are they doing with the lantern out on the battery?

CAPTAIN. Do you see a lantern?

CURT. Yes, and people moving about.

CAPTAIN. I suppose it is what we call a service squad.

CURT. What is that?

CAPTAIN. A few men and a corporal. Probably some poor wretch that has to be locked up.

CURT. Oh!   [*Pause.*

CAPTAIN. Now, when you know Alice, how do you like her?

CURT. I cannot tell— I have no understanding of people at all. She is as inexplicable to me as you are, or as I am myself. For I am reaching the age when wisdom makes this acknowledgment: I know nothing, I understand nothing! But when I observe an action, I like to get at the motive behind it. Why did you push her into the water?

CAPTAIN. I don't know. It merely seemed quite natural to me, as she was standing on the pier, that she ought to be in the water.

CURT. Have you ever regretted it?

CAPTAIN. Never!

CURT. That's strange!

CAPTAIN. Of course, it is! So strange that I cannot realise that I am the man who has been guilty of such a mean act.

CURT. Have you not expected her to take some revenge?

CAPTAIN. Well, she seems to have taken it in full measure; and that, too, seems no less natural to me.

CURT. What has so suddenly brought you to this cynical resignation?

CAPTAIN. Since I looked death in the face, life has presented itself from a different viewpoint. Tell me, if you were to judge between Alice and myself, whom would you place in the right?

CURT. Neither of you. But to both of you I should give endless compassion—perhaps a little more of it to you!

CAPTAIN. Give me your hand, Curt!

CURT. [*Gives him one hand and puts the other one on the* CAPTAIN's *shoulder*] Old boy!

ALICE. [*In from the left, carrying a sunshade*] Well, how harmonious! Oh, friendship! Has there been no telegram yet?

CURT. [*Coldly*] No.

ALICE. This delay makes me impatient, and when I grow impatient I push matters along— Look, Curt, how I give him the final bullet. And now he'll bite the grass! First, I load— I know all about rifle practice, the famous rifle practice of which less than 5,000 copies were sold—and then I aim—fire! [*She takes aim with her sunshade*] How is your new wife? The young, beautiful, unknown one? You don't know! But I know how my lover is doing. [*Puts her arms around the neck of* CURT *and kisses him; he thrusts her away from himself*] He is well, although still a little bashful! You wretch, whom I have never loved—you, who were too conceited to be jealous—you never saw how I was leading you by the nose!

> The CAPTAIN *draws the sabre and makes a leap at her,* *aiming at her several futile blows that only hit the* *furniture.*

ALICE. Help! Help!

> [CURT *does not move.*

CAPTAIN. [*Falls with the sabre in his hand*] Judith, avenge me!

ALICE. Hooray! He's dead!

[*Curt withdraws toward the door in the background.*

CAPTAIN. [*Gets on his feet*] Not yet! [*Sheathes the sabre and sits down in the easy-chair by the sewing-table*] Judith! Judith!

ALICE. [*Drawing nearer to* CURT] Now I go—with you!

CURT. [*Pushes her back with such force that she sinks to her knees*] Go back to the hell whence you came! Good-bye for ever!   [*Goes to the door.*

CAPTAIN. Don't leave me Curt; she will kill me!

ALICE. Don't desert me, Curt—don't desert us!

CURT. Good-bye!   [*Goes out.*

ALICE. [*With a sudden change of attitude*] The wretch! That's a friend for you!

CAPTAIN. [*Softly*] Forgive me, Alice, and come here—come quick!

ALICE. [*Over to the* CAPTAIN] That's the worst rascal and hypocrite I have met in my life! Do you know, you are a man after all!

CAPTAIN. Listen, Alice! I cannot live much longer.

ALICE. Is that so?

CAPTAIN. The doctor has said so.

ALICE. Then there was no truth in the rest either?

CAPTAIN. No.

ALICE. [*In despair*] Oh, what have I done!

CAPTAIN. There is help for everything.

ALICE. No, this is beyond helping!

CAPTAIN. Nothing is beyond helping, if you only wipe it out and pass on.

ALICE. But the telegram—the telegram!

CAPTAIN. Which telegram?

ALICE. [*On her knees beside the* CAPTAIN] Are we then cast out? Must this happen? I have sprung a mine under myself, under us. Why did you have to tell untruths? And why should that man come here to tempt me? We are lost! Your magnanimity might have helped everything, forgiven everything!

CAPTAIN. What is it that cannot be forgiven? What is it that I have not already forgiven you?

ALICE. You are right—but there is no help for this.

CAPTAIN. I cannot guess it, although I know your ingenuity when it comes to villanies——

ALICE. Oh, if I could only get out of this, I should care for you— I should love you, Edgar!

CAPTAIN. Listen to me! Where do I stand?

ALICE. Don't you think anybody can help us—well, no man can!

CAPTAIN. Who could then help?

ALICE. [*Looking the* CAPTAIN *straight in the eye*] I don't know— Think of it, what is to become of the children with their name dishonoured——?

CAPTAIN. Have you dishonoured that name?

ALICE. Not I! Not I! And then they must leave school! And as they go out into the world, they will be lonely as we, and cruel as we— Then you didn't meet Judith either, I understand now?

CAPTAIN. No, but wipe it out!

The telegraph receiver clicks. ALICE *flies up.*

ALICE. [*Screams*] Now ruin is overtaking us! [*To the* CAPTAIN] Don't listen!

CAPTAIN. [*Quietly*] I am not going to listen, dear child—just calm yourself!

ALICE. [*Standing by the instrument, raises herself on tip-*

toe in order to look out through the window] Don't listen!
Don't listen!

CAPTAIN. [*Holding his hands over his ears*] Lisa, child, I
am stopping up my ears.

ALICE. [*On her knees, with lifted hands*] God, help us!
The squad is coming— [*Weeping and sobbing*] God in heaven!

> *She appears to be moving her lips as if in silent prayer.*
> *The telegraph receiver continues to click for a while and*
> *a long white strip of paper seems to crawl out of the*
> *instrument.   Then complete silence prevails once more.*

ALICE. [*Rises, tears off the paper strip, and reads it in silence.*
Then she turns her eyes upward for a moment.   Goes over
to the CAPTAIN *and kisses him on the forehead*] That is over
now!   It was nothing!

> *Sits down in the other chair, puts her handkerchief to*
> *her face, and breaks into a violent spell of weeping.*

CAPTAIN. What kind of secrets are these?

ALICE. Don't ask!   It is over now!

CAPTAIN. As you please, child.

ALICE. You would not have spoken like that three days
ago—what has done it?

CAPTAIN. Well, dear, when I fell down that first time, I
went a little way on the other side of the grave.   What I saw
has been forgotten. but the impression of it still remains.

ALICE. And it was?

CAPTAIN. A hope—for something better!

ALICE. Something better?

CAPTAIN. Yes.   That this could be the real life, I have, in
fact, never believed: it is death—or something still worse!

ALICE. And we——

CAPTAIN. Have probably been set to torment each other—
so it seems at least!

ALICE. Have we tormented each other enough?

CAPTAIN. Yes, I think so! And upset things! [*Looks around*] Suppose we put things to rights? And clean house?

ALICE. Yes, if it can be done.

CAPTAIN. [*Gets up to survey the room*] It can't be done in one day—no, it can't!

ALICE. In two, then! Many days!

CAPTAIN. Let us hope so! [*Pause. Sits down again*] So you didn't get free this time after all! But then, you didn't get me locked up either! [ALICE *looks staggered*] Yes, I know you wanted to put me in prison, but I wipe it out. I suppose you have done worse than that— [ALICE *is speechless*] And I was innocent of those defalcations.

ALICE. And now you intend me to become your nurse?

CAPTAIN. If you are willing!

ALICE. What else could I do?

CAPTAIN. I don't know!

ALICE. [*Sits down, numbed and crushed*] These are the eternal torments! Is there, then, no end to them?

CAPTAIN. Yes, if we are patient. Perhaps life begins when death comes.

ALICE. If it were so!   [*Pause.*

CAPTAIN. You think Curt a hypocrite?

ALICE. Of course I do!

CAPTAIN. And I don't! But all who come near us turn evil and go their way. Curt was weak, and the evil is strong! [*Pause*] How commonplace life has become! Formerly blows were struck; now you shake your fist at the most! I am fairly certain that, three months from now, we shall celebrate our silver wedding—with Curt as best man—and with the Doctor and Gerda among the guests. The Quartermaster will make the speech and the Sergeant-Major will lead the cheering. And if I know the Colonel right, he will come on his own invitation— Yes, you may laugh! But do you recall the silver wedding of Adolph—in the Fusiliers? The bride had to carry her wedding ring on the right hand, because the groom in a tender moment had chopped off her left ring finger with his dirk. [ALICE *puts her handkerchief to her mouth in order to repress her laughter*] Are you crying? No, I believe you are laughing! Yes, child, partly we weep and partly we laugh. Which is the right thing to do?—Don't ask me! The other day I read in a newspaper that a man had been divorced seven times—which means that he had been married seven times—and finally, at the age of ninety-eight, he ran away with his first wife and married her again. Such is love! If life be serious, or merely a joke, is more than I can decide. Often it is most painful when a joke, and its seriousness is after all more agreeable and peaceful. But when at last you try to be serious, somebody comes and plays a joke on you—as Curt, for instance! Do you want a silver wedding? [ALICE *remains silent*] Oh, say yes! They will laugh at us, but what does it matter? We may laugh also, or keep serious, as the occasion may require.

ALICE. Well, all right!

CAPTAIN. Silver wedding, then! [*Rising*] Wipe out and pass on! Therefore, let us pass on!

Curtain.

THE DANCE OF DEATH

PART II

CHARACTERS

EDGAR

ALICE

CURT

ALLAN, *the son of* CURT

JUDITH, *the daughter of* EDGAR

THE LIEUTENANT

THE DANCE OF DEATH

PART II

A rectangular drawing-room in white and gold. The rear wall is broken by several French windows reaching down to the floor. These stand open, revealing a garden terrace outside. Along this terrace, serving as a public promenade, runs a stone balustrade, on which are ranged pots of blue and white faïence, with petunias and scarlet geraniums in them. Beyond, in the background, can be seen the shore battery with a sentry pacing back and forth. In the far distance, the open sea.

At the left of the drawing-room stands a sofa with gilded woodwork. In front of it are a table and chairs. At the right is a grand piano, a writing-table, and an open fireplace.

In the foreground, an American easy-chair.

By the writing-table is a standing lamp of copper with a table attached to it.

On the walls are several old-fashioned oil paintings.

> ALLAN *is sitting at the writing-table, engrossed in some mathematical problem.* JUDITH *enters from the background, in summer dress, short skirt, hair in a braid down her back, hat in one hand and tennis racket in the other. She stops in the doorway.* ALLAN *rises, serious and respectful.*

JUDITH. [*In serious but friendly tone*] Why don't you come and play tennis?

ALLAN. [*Bashful, struggling with his emotion*] I am very busy——

219

JUDITH. Didn't you see that I had made my bicycle point toward the oak, and not away from it?

ALLAN. Yes, I saw it.

JUDITH. Well, what does it mean?

ALLAN. It means—that you want me to come and play tennis—but my duty—I have some problems to work out—and your father is a rather exacting teacher——

JUDITH. Do you like him?   .

ALLAN. Yes, I do. He takes such interest in all his pupils——

JUDITH. He takes an interest in everything and every-body. Won't you come?

ALLAN. You know I should like to—but I must not!

JUDITH. I'll ask papa to give you leave.

ALLAN. Don't do that. It will only cause talk.

JUDITH. Don't you think I can manage him? He wants what I want.

ALLAN. I suppose that is because you are so hard.

JUDITH. You should be hard also.

ALLAN. I don't belong to the wolf family.

JUDITH. Then you are a sheep.

ALLAN. Rather that.

JUDITH. Tell me why you don't want to come and play tennis?

ALLAN. You know it.

JUDITH. Tell me anyhow. The Lieutenant——

ALLAN. Yes, you don't care for me at all, but you cannot enjoy yourself with the Lieutenant unless I am present, so you can see me suffer.

JUDITH. Am I as cruel as that? I didn't know it.

ALLAN. Well, now you know it.

JUDITH. Then I shall do better hereafter, for I don't want to be cruel, I don't want to be bad—in your eyes.

ALLAN. You say this only to fasten your hold on me. I am already your slave, but it does not satisfy you. The slave must be tortured and thrown to the wild beasts. You have already that other fellow in your clutches—what do you want with me then? Let me go my own way, and you can go yours.

JUDITH. Do you send me away? [ALLAN *does not answer*] Then I go! As second cousins, we shall have to meet now and then, but I am not going to bother you any longer.

[ALLAN *sits down at the table and returns to his problem.*

JUDITH. [*Instead of going away, comes down the stage and approaches gradually the table where* ALLAN *is sitting*] Don't be afraid, I am going at once— I wanted only to see how the Master of Quarantine lives— [*Looks around*] White and gold —a Bechstein grand—well, well! We are still in the fort since papa was pensioned—in the tower where mamma has been kept twenty-five years—and we are there on sufferance at that. You—you are rich——

ALLAN. [*Calmly*] We are not rich.

JUDITH. So you say, but you are always wearing fine clothes —but whatever you wear, for that matter, is becoming to you. Do you hear what I say? [*Drawing nearer.*

ALLAN. [*Submissively*] I do.

JUDITH. How can you hear when you keep on figuring, or whatever you are doing?

ALLAN. I don't use my eyes to listen with.

JUDITH. Your eyes—have you ever looked at them in the mirror?

ALLAN. Go away!

JUDITH. You despise me, do you?

ALLAN. Why, girl, I am not thinking of you at all.

JUDITH. [*Still nearer*] Archimedes is deep in his figures when the soldier comes and cuts him down.

[*Stirs his papers about with the racket.*

ALLAN. Don't touch my papers!

JUDITH. That's what Archimedes said also. Now you are thinking something foolish—you are thinking that I can not live without you——

ALLAN. Why can't you leave me alone?

JUDITH. Be courteous, and I'll help you with your examinations——

ALLAN. You?

JUDITH. Yes, I know the examiners——

ALLAN. [*Sternly*] And what of it?

JUDITH. Don't you know that one should stand well with the teachers?

ALLAN. Do you mean your father and the Lieutenant?

JUDITH. And the Colonel!

ALLAN. And then you mean that your protection would enable me to shirk my work?

JUDITH. You are a bad translator——

ALLAN. Of a bad original——

JUDITH. Be ashamed!

ALLAN. So I am—both on your behalf and my own! I am ashamed of having listened to you— Why don't you go?

JUDITH. Because I know you appreciate my company— Yes, you manage always to pass by my window. You have always some errand that brings you into the city with the same boat that I take. You cannot go for a sail without having me to look after the jib.

ALLAN. But a young girl shouldn't say that kind of things!

JUDITH. Do you mean to say that I am a child?

ALLAN. Sometimes you are a good child, and sometimes a bad woman. Me you seem to have picked to be your sheep.

JUDITH. You are a sheep, and that's why I am going to protect you.

ALLAN. [*Rising*] The wolf makes a poor shepherd! You want to eat me—that is the secret of it, I suppose. You want to put your beautiful eyes in pawn to get possession of my head.

JUDITH. Oh, you have been looking at my eyes? I didn't expect that much courage of you.

> ALLAN *collects his papers and starts to go out toward the right.*

> JUDITH *places herself in front of the door.*

ALLAN. Get out of my way, or——

JUDITH. Or?

ALLAN. If you were a boy—bah! But you are a girl.

JUDITH. And then?

ALLAN. If you had any pride at all, you would be gone, as you may regard yourself as shown the door.

JUDITH. I'll get back at you for that!

ALLAN. I don't doubt it!

JUDITH. [*Goes enraged toward the background*] I—shall—get—back—at you for that!   [*Goes out.*

CURT. [*Enters from the left*] Where are you going, Allan?

ALLAN. Oh, is that you?

CURT. Who was it that left in such hurry—so that the bushes shook?

ALLAN. It was Judith.

CURT. She is a little impetuous, but a fine girl.

ALLAN. When a girl is cruel and rude, she is always said to be a fine girl.

CURT. Don't be so severe, Allan! Are you not satisfied with your new relatives?

ALLAN. I like Uncle Edgar——

CURT. Yes, he has many good sides. How about your other teachers—the Lieutenant, for instance?

ALLAN. He's so uncertain. Sometimes he seems to have a grudge against me.

CURT. Oh, no! You just go here and make people "seem" this or that. Don't brood, but look after your own affairs, do what is proper, and leave others to their own concerns.

ALLAN. So I do, but—they won't leave me alone. They pull you in—as the cuttlefish down at the landing—they don't bite, but they stir up vortices that suck——

CURT. You have some tendency to melancholia, I think. Don't you feel at home here with me? Is there anything you miss?

ALLAN. I have never been better off, but—there is something here that smothers me.

CURT. Here by the sea? Are you not fond of the sea?

ALLAN. Yes, the open sea. But along the shores you find eelgrass, cuttlefish, jellyfish, sea-nettles, or whatever they are called.

CURT. You shouldn't stay indoors so much. Go out and play tennis.

ALLAN. Oh, that's no fun!

CURT. You are angry with Judith, I guess?

ALLAN. Judith?

CURT. You are so exacting toward people—it is not wise, for then you become isolated.

ALLAN. I am not exacting, but— It feels as if I were lying at the bottom of a pile of wood and had to wait my turn to get into the fire—and it weighs on me—all that is above weighs me down.

CURT. Bide your turn. The pile grows smaller——

ALLAN. Yes, but so slowly, so slowly. And in the meantime I lie here and grow mouldy.

CURT. It is not pleasant to be young. And yet you young ones are envied.

ALLAN. Are we? Would you change?

CURT. No, thanks!

ALLAN. Do you know what is worse than anything else? It is to sit still and keep silent while the old ones talk nonsense—I know that I am better informed than they on some matters—and yet I must keep silent. Well, pardon me, I am not counting you among the old.

CURT. Why not?

ALLAN. Perhaps because we have only just now become acquainted——

CURT. And because—your ideas of me have undergone a change?

ALLAN. Yes.

CURT. During the years we were separated, I suppose you didn't always think of me in a friendly way?

ALLAN. No.

CURT. Did you ever see a picture of me?

ALLAN. One, and it was very unfavourable.

CURT. And old-looking?

ALLAN. Yes.

CURT. Ten years ago my hair turned gray in a single night —it has since then resumed its natural color without my doing anything for it— Let us talk of something else! There comes your aunt—my cousin. How do you like her?

ALLAN. I don't want to tell!

CURT. Then I shall not ask you.

ALICE. [*Enters dressed in a very light-colored walking-suit and carrying a sunshade*] Good morning, Curt.

[*Gives him a glance signifying that* ALLAN *should leave.*

CURT. [*To* ALLAN] Leave us, please.

ALLAN *goes out to the right.*

ALICE *takes a seat on the sofa to the left.*

CURT *sits down on a chair near her.*

ALICE. [*In some confusion*] He will be here in a moment, so you need not feel embarrassed.

CURT. And why should I?

ALICE. You, with your strictness——

CURT. Toward myself, yes——

ALICE. Of course— Once I forgot myself, when in you I saw the liberator, but you kept your self-control—and for that reason we have a right to forget—what has never been.

CURT. Forget it then!

ALICE. However— I don't think *he* has forgotten——

CURT. You are thinking of that night when his heart gave out and he fell on the floor—and when you rejoiced too quickly, thinking him already dead?

ALICE. Yes. Since then he has recovered; but when he gave up drinking, he learned to keep silent, and now he is terrible. He is up to something that I cannot make out——

CURT. Your husband, Alice, is a harmless fool who has shown me all sorts of kindnesses——

ALICE. Beware of his kindnesses. I know them.

CURT. Well, well——

ALICE. He has then blinded you also? Can you not see the danger? Don't you notice the snares?

CURT. No.

ALICE. Then your ruin is certain.

CURT. Oh, mercy!

ALICE. Think only, I have to sit here and see disaster stalking you like a cat—I point at it, but you cannot see it.

CURT. Allan, with his unspoiled vision, cannot see it either. He sees nothing but Judith, for that matter, and this seems to me a safeguard of our good relationship.

ALICE. Do you know Judith?

CURT. A flirtatious little thing, with a braid down her back and rather too short skirts——

ALICE. Exactly! But the other day I saw her dressed up in long skirts—and then she was a young lady—and not so very young either, when her hair was put up.

CURT. She is somewhat precocious, I admit.

ALICE. And she is playing with Allan.

CURT. That's all right, so long as it remains play.

ALICE. So *that* is all right?— Now Edgar will be here soon, and he will take the easy-chair—he loves it with such passion that he could steal it.

CURT. Why, he can have it!

ALICE. Let him sit over there, and we'll stay here. And when he talks—he is always talkative in the morning—when he talks of insignificant things, I'll translate them for you——

CURT. Oh, my dear Alice, you are too deep, far too deep. What could I have to fear as long as I look after my quarantine properly and otherwise behave decently?

ALICE. You believe in justice and honour and all that sort of thing.

CURT. Yes, and it is what experience has taught me. Once I believed the very opposite—and paid dearly for it!

ALICE. Now he's coming!

CURT. I have never seen you so frightened before.

ALICE. My bravery was nothing but ignorance of the danger.

CURT. Danger? Soon you'll have me frightened too!

ALICE. Oh, if I only could— There!

> The CAPTAIN *enters from the background, in civilian dress, black Prince Albert buttoned all the way, military cap, and a cane with silver handle. He greets them with a nod and goes straight to the easy-chair, where he sits down.*

ALICE. [*To* CURT] Let him speak first.

CAPTAIN. This is a splendid chair you have here, dear Curt; perfectly splendid.

CURT. I'll give it to you, if you will accept it.

CAPTAIN. That was not what I meant——

CURT. But I mean it seriously. How much have I not received from you?

CAPTAIN. [*Garrulously*] Oh, nonsense! And when I sit here, I can overlook the whole island, all the walks; I can see all the people on their verandahs, all the ships on the sea, that are coming in and going out. You have really happened on the best piece of this island, which is certainly not an island of the blessed. Or what do you say, Alice? Yes, they call it "Little Hell," and here Curt has built himself a paradise, but without an Eve, of course, for when she appeared, then the paradise came to an end. I say—do you know that this was a royal hunting lodge?

CURT. So I have heard.

CAPTAIN. You live royally, you, but, if I may say so myself, you have me to thank for it.

ALICE. [*To* CURT] There—now he wants to steal you.

CURT. I have to thank you for a good deal.

CAPTAIN. Fudge! Tell me, did you get the wine cases?

CURT. Yes.

CAPTAIN. And you are satisfied?

CURT. Quite satisfied, and you may tell your dealer so.

CAPTAIN. His goods are always prime quality——

ALICE. [*To* CURT] At second-rate prices, and you have to pay the difference.

CAPTAIN. What did you say, Alice?

ALICE. I? Nothing!

CAPTAIN. Well, when this quarantine station was about to be established, I had in mind applying for the position—and so I made a study of quarantine methods.

ALICE. [*To* CURT] Now he's lying!

CAPTAIN. [*Boastfully*] And I did not share the antiquated ideas concerning disinfection which were then accepted by the government.   For I placed myself on the side of the Neptunists —so called because they emphasise the use of water——

CURT. Beg your pardon, but I remember distinctly that it was I who preached water, and you fire, at that time.

CAPTAIN. I? Nonsense!

ALICE. [*Aloud*] Yes, I remember that, too.

CAPTAIN. You?

CURT. I remember it so much the better because——

CAPTAIN. [*Cutting him short*] Well, it's possible, but it does not matter.   [*Raising his voice*] However—we have now reached a point where a new state of affairs—[*To* CURT, *who wants to interrupt*] just a moment!—has begun to prevail— and when the methods of quarantining are about to become revolutionized.

CURT. By the by, do you know who is writing those stupid articles in that periodical?

CAPTAIN. [*Flushing*] No, I don't know, but why do you call them stupid?

ALICE. [*To* CURT] Look out!   It is he who writes them.

CURT. He?— [*To the* CAPTAIN] Not very well advised, at least.

CAPTAIN. Well, are you the man to judge of that?

ALICE. Are we going to have a quarrel?

CURT. Not at all.

CAPTAIN. It is hard to keep peace on this island, but we ought to set a good example——

CURT. Yes, can you explain this to me?   When I came here I made friends with all the officials and became especially intimate with the regimental auditor—as intimate as men are likely to become at our age.   And then, in a little while—it was shortly after your recovery—one after another began to grow cold toward me—and yesterday the auditor avoided me on the promenade.   I cannot tell you how it hurt me!   [*The* CAPTAIN *remains silent*]   Have you noticed any ill-feeling toward yourself?

CAPTAIN. No, on the contrary.

ALICE. [*To* CURT] Don't you understand that he has been stealing your friends?

CURT. [*To the* CAPTAIN] I wondered whether it might have anything to do with this new stock issue to which I refused to subscribe.

CAPTAIN. No, no—   But can you tell me why you didn't subscribe?

CURT. Because I have already put my small savings into your soda factory.   And also because a new issue means that the old stock is shaky.

CAPTAIN. [*Preoccupied*] That's a splendid lamp you have. Where did you get it?

CURT. In the city, of course.

ALICE. [*To* CURT] Look out for your lamp!

CURT. [*To the* CAPTAIN] You must not think that I am ungrateful or distrustful, Edgar.

CAPTAIN. No, but it shows small confidence to withdraw from an undertaking which you have helped to start.

CURT. Why, ordinary prudence bids everybody save himself and what is his.

CAPTAIN. Save?   Is there any danger then?   Do you think anybody wants to rob you?

CURT. Why such sharp words?

CAPTAIN. Were you not satisfied when I helped you to place your money at six per cent.?

CURT. Yes, and even grateful.

CAPTAIN. You are not grateful—it is not in your nature, but this you cannot help.

ALICE. [*To* CURT] Listen to him!

CURT. My nature has shortcomings enough, and my struggle against them has not been very successful, but I do recognise obligations——

CAPTAIN. Show it then! [*Reaches out his hand to pick up a newspaper*] Why, what is this? A death notice? [*Reads*] The Health Commissioner is dead.

ALICE. [*To* CURT] Now he is speculating in the corpse——

CAPTAIN. [*As if to himself*] This is going to bring about certain—changes——

CURT. In what respect?

CAPTAIN. [*Rising*] That remains to be seen.

ALICE. [*To the* CAPTAIN] Where are you going?

CAPTAIN. I think I'll have to go to the city— [*Catches sight of a letter on the writing-table, picks it up as if unconsciously, reads the address, and puts it back*] Oh, I hope you will pardon my absent-mindedness.

CURT. No harm done.

CAPTAIN. Why, that's Allan's drawing case. Where is the boy?

CURT. He is out playing with the girls.

CAPTAIN. That big boy? I don't like it. And Judith must not be running about like that. You had better keep an eye on your young gentleman, and I'll look after my young lady. [*Goes over to the piano and strikes a few notes*] Splendid tone in this instrument. A Steinbech, isn't it?

CURT. A Bechstein.

CAPTAIN. Yes, you are well fixed. Thank me for bringing you here.

ALICE. [*To* CURT] He lies, for he tried to keep you away.

CAPTAIN. Well, good-bye for a while. I am going to take the next boat.

[*Scrutinises the paintings on the walls as he goes out.*

ALICE. Well?

CURT. Well?

ALICE. I can't see through his plans yet. But—tell me one thing. This envelope he looked at—from whom is the letter?

CURT. I am sorry to admit—it was my one secret.

ALICE. And he ferreted it out. Can you see that he knows witchery, as I have told you before? Is there anything printed on the envelope?

CURT. Yes—"The Citizens' Union."

ALICE. Then he has guessed your secret. You want to get into the Riksdag, I suppose. And now you'll see that he goes there instead of you.

CURT. Has he ever thought of it?

ALICE. No, but he is thinking of it now. I read it on his face while he was looking at the envelope.

CURT. That's why he has to go to the city?

ALICE. No, he made up his mind to go when he read the death notice.

CURT. What has he to gain by the death of the Health Commissioner?

ALICE. Hard to tell! Perhaps the man was an enemy who had stood in the way of his plans.

CURT. If he be as terrible as you say, then there is reason to fear him.

ALICE. Didn't you hear how he wanted to steal you, to tie your hands by means of pretended obligations that do not exist? For instance, he has done nothing to get you this position, but has, on the contrary, tried to keep you out of it. He is a man-thief, an insect, one of those wood-borers that eat up your insides so that one day you find yourself as hollow as a dying pine tree. He hates you, although he is bound to you by the memory of your youthful friendship——

CURT. How keen-witted we are made by our hatreds!

ALICE. And stupid by our loves—blind and stupid!

CURT. Oh, no, don't say that!

ALICE. Do you know what is meant by a vampire? They say it is the soul of a dead person seeking a body in which it may live as a parasite. Edgar is dead—ever since he fell down on the floor that time. You see, he has no interests of his own, no personality, no initiative. But if he can only get hold of some other person he hangs on to him, sends down roots into him, and begins to flourish and blossom. Now he has fastened himself on you.

CURT. If he comes too close I'll shake him off.

ALICE. Try to shake off a burr! Listen: do you know why he does not want Judith and Allan to play?

CURT. I suppose he is concerned about their feelings.

ALICE. Not at all. He wants to marry Judith to—the Colonel!

CURT. [Shocked] That old widower!

ALICE. Yes.

CURT. Horrible! And Judith?

ALICE. If she could get the General, who is eighty, she would take him in order to bully the Colonel, who is sixty. To bully, you know, that's the aim of her life. To trample down and bully—there you have the motto of that family.

CURT. Can this be Judith? That maiden fair and proud and splendid?

ALICE. Oh, I know all about that! May I sit here and write a letter?

CURT. [Puts the writing-table in order] With pleasure.

ALICE. [Takes off her gloves and sits down at the writing-

table] Now we'll try our hand at the art of war.   I failed once when I tried to slay my dragon.   But now I have mastered the trade.

CURT. Do you know that it is necessary to load before you fire?

ALICE. Yes, and with ball cartridges at that!

> CURT *withdraws to the right.*

> ALICE *ponders and writes.*

> ALLAN *comes rushing in without noticing* ALICE *and throws himself face downward on the sofa.   He is weeping convulsively into a lace handkerchief.*

ALICE. [*Watches him for a while.   Then she rises and goes over to the sofa.   Speaks in a tender voice*] Allan!

> ALLAN *sits up disconcertedly and hides the handkerchief behind his back.*

ALICE. [*Tenderly, womanly, and with true emotion*] You should not be afraid of me, Allan—   I am not dangerous to you—   What is wrong?   Are you sick?

ALLAN. Yes.

ALICE. In what way?

ALLAN. I don't know.

ALICE. Have you a headache?

ALLAN. No.

ALICE. And your chest?   Pain?

ALLAN. Yes.

ALICE. Pain—pain—as if your heart wanted to melt away. And it pulls, pulls——

ALLAN. How do you know?

ALICE. And then you wish to die—that you were already dead—and everything seems so hard.   And you can only think of one thing—always the same—but if two are thinking of the same thing, then sorrow falls heavily on one of them. [ALLAN *forgets himself and begins to pick at the handkerchief*]

That's the sickness which no one can cure. You cannot
eat and you cannot drink; you want only to weep, and you
weep so bitterly—especially out in the woods where nobody
can see you, for at that kind of sorrow all men laugh—men
who are so cruel! Dear me! What do you want of her?
Nothing! You don't want to kiss her mouth, for you feel
that you would die if you did. When your thoughts run to
her, you feel as if death were approaching. And it is death,
child—that sort of death—which brings life. But you don't
understand it yet! I smell violets—it is herself. [*Steps
closer to* ALLAN *and takes the handkerchief gently away from
him*] It is she, it is she everywhere, none but she! Oh, oh,
oh! [ALLAN *cannot help burying his face in* ALICE'S *bosom*]
Poor boy! Poor boy! Oh, how it hurts, how it hurts!
[*Wipes off his tears with the handkerchief*] There, there! Cry
—cry to your heart's content. There now! Then the heart
grows lighter— But now, Allan, rise up and be a man, or
she will not look at you—she, the cruel one, who is not cruel. .
Has she tormented you? With the Lieutenant? You must
make friends with the Lieutenant, so that you two can talk
of her. That gives a little ease also.

ALLAN. I don't want to see the Lieutenant!

ALICE. Now look here, little boy, it won't be long before the
Lieutenant seeks you out in order to get a chance to talk of
her. For— [ALLAN *looks up with a ray of hope on his face*]
Well, shall I be nice and tell you? [ALLAN *droops his head*] He
is just as unhappy as you are.

ALLAN. [*Happy*] No?

ALICE. Yes, indeed, and he needs somebody to whom he
may unburden his heart when Judith has wounded him.
You seem to rejoice in advance?

ALLAN. Does she not want the Lieutenant?

ALICE. She does not want you either, dear boy, for she

wants the Colonel. [ALLAN *is saddened again*] Is it raining again? Well, the handkerchief you cannot have, for Judith is careful about her belongings and wants her dozen complete. [ALLAN *looks dashed*] Yes, my boy, such is Judith. Sit over there now, while I write another letter, and then you may do an errand for me.

[*Sits down at the writing-table and begins to write again.*

LIEUTENANT. [*Enters from the background, with a melancholy face, but without being ridiculous. Without noticing* ALICE *he makes straight for* ALLAN] I say, Cadet— [ALLAN *rises and stands at attention*] Please be seated.

> ALICE *watches them.*

> The LIEUTENANT *goes up to* ALLAN *and sits down beside him. Sighs, takes out a lace handkerchief just like the other one, and wipes his forehead with it.*
> ALLAN *stares greedily at the handkerchief.*
> The LIEUTENANT *looks sadly at* ALLAN.
> ALICE *coughs.*
> The LIEUTENANT *jumps up and stands at attention.*

ALICE. Please be seated.

LIEUTENANT. I beg your pardon, madam——

ALICE. Never mind! Please sit down and keep the Cadet company—he is feeling a little lonely here on the island.

[*Writes.*

LIEUTENANT. [*Conversing with* ALLAN *in low tone and uneasily*] It is awfully hot.

ALLAN. Rather.

LIEUTENANT. Have you finished the sixth book yet?

ALLAN. I have just got to the last proposition.

LIEUTENANT. That's a tough one. [*Silence*] Have you— [*seeking for words*] played tennis to-day?

ALLAN. No-o—the sun was too hot.

LIEUTENANT. [*In despair, but without any comical effect*] Yes, it's awfully hot to-day!

ALLAN. [*In a whisper*] Yes, it is very hot.   [*Silence.*

LIEUTENANT. Have you—been out sailing to-day?

ALLAN. No-o, I couldn't get anybody to tend the jib.

LIEUTENANT. Could you—trust me sufficiently to let me tend the jib?

ALLAN. [*Respectfully as before*] That would be too great an honor for me, Lieutenant.

LIEUTENANT. Not at all, not at all! Do you think—the wind might be good enough to-day—about dinner-time, say, for that's the only time I am free?

ALLAN. [*Slyly*] It always calms down about dinner-time, and—that's the time Miss Judith has her lesson.

LIEUTENANT. [*Sadly*] Oh, yes, yes! Hm! Do you think——

ALICE. Would one of you young gentlemen care to deliver a letter for me? [ALLAN *and the* LIEUTENANT *exchange glances of mutual distrust*] —to Miss Judith? [ALLAN *and the* LIEUTENANT *jump up and hasten over to* ALICE, *but not without a certain dignity meant to disguise their emotion*] Both of you? Well, the more safely my errand will be attended to. [*Hands the letter to the* LIEUTENANT] If you please, Lieutenant, I should like to have that handkerchief. My daughter is very careful about her things—there is a touch of pettiness in her nature— Give me that handkerchief! I don't wish to laugh at you, but you must not make yourself ridiculous— needlessly. And the Colonel does not like to play the part of an Othello. [*Takes the handkerchief*] Away with you now, young men, and try to hide your feelings as much as you can.

> *The* LIEUTENANT *bows and goes out, followed closely by* ALLAN.

ALICE. [*Calls out*] Allan!

ALLAN. [*Stops unwillingly in the doorway*] Yes, Aunt.

ALICE. Stay here, unless you want to inflict more suffering on yourself than you can bear.

ALLAN. But he is going!

ALICE. Let him burn himself. But take care of yourself.

ALLAN. I don't want to take care of myself.

ALICE. And then you cry afterward. And so I get the trouble of consoling you.

ALLAN. I want to go!

ALICE. Go then! But come back here, young madcap, and I'll have the right to laugh at you.

> [ALLAN *runs after the* LIEUTENANT.
>
> [ALICE *writes again.*

CURT. [*Enters*] Alice, I have received an anonymous letter that is bothering me.

ALICE. Have you noticed that Edgar has become another person since he put off the uniform? I could never have believed that a coat might make such a difference.

CURT. You didn't answer my question.

ALICE. It was no question. It was a piece of information. What do you fear?

CURT. Everything!

ALICE. He went to the city. And his trips to the city are always followed by something dreadful.

CURT. But I can do nothing because I don't know from which quarter the attack will begin.

ALICE. [*Folding the letter*] We'll see whether I have guessed it.

CURT. Will you help me then?

ALICE. Yes—but no further than my own interests permit. My own—that is my children's.

CURT. I understand that! Do you hear how silent everything is—here on land, out on the sea, everywhere?

ALICE. But behind the silence I hear voices—mutterings, cries!

CURT. Hush! I hear something, too—no, it was only the gulls.

ALICE. But I hear something else! And now I am going to the post-office—with this letter!

Curtain.

Same stage setting. ALLAN *is sitting at the writing-table study-
ing.* JUDITH *is standing in the doorway. She wears a
tennis hat and carries the handle-bars of a bicycle in one
hand.*

JUDITH. Can I borrow your wrench?

ALLAN. [*Without looking up*] No, you cannot.

JUDITH. You are discourteous now, because you think I
am running after you.

ALLAN. [*Without crossness*] I am nothing at all, but I ask
merely to be left alone.

JUDITH. [*Comes nearer*] Allan!

ALLAN. Yes, what is it?

JUDITH. You mustn't be angry with me!

ALLAN. I am not.

JUDITH. Will you give me your hand on that?

ALLAN. [*Kindly*] I don't want to shake hands with you,
but I am not angry— What do you want with me anyhow?

JUDITH. Oh, but you're stupid!

ALLAN. Well, let it go at that.

JUDITH. You think me cruel, and nothing else.

ALLAN. No, for I know that you are kind too—you *can* be
kind!

JUDITH. Well—how can I help—that you and the Lieutenant run around and weep in the woods? Tell me, why
do you weep? [ALLAN *is embarrassed*] Tell me now— I never
weep. And why have you become such good friends? Of
what do you talk while you are walking about arm in arm?
[ALLAN *cannot answer*] Allan, you'll soon see what kind I am
and whether I can strike a blow for one I like. And I want
240

to give you a piece of advice—although I have no use for tale-bearing. Be prepared!

ALLAN. For what?

JUDITH. Trouble.

ALLAN. From what quarter?

JUDITH. From the quarter where you least expect it.

ALLAN. Well, I am rather used to disappointment, and life has not brought me much that was pleasant What's in store now?

JUDITH. [*Pensively*] You poor boy—give me your hand! [ALLAN *gives her his hand*] Look at me! Don't you dare to look at me?

[ALLAN *rushes out to the left in order to hide his emotion.*

LIEUTENANT. [*In from the background*] I beg your pardon! I thought that——

JUDITH. Tell me, Lieutenant, will you be my friend and ally?

LIEUTENANT. If you'll do me the honour——

JUDITH. Yes—a word only—don't desert Allan when disaster overtakes him.

LIEUTENANT. What disaster?

JUDITH. You'll soon see—this very day perhaps. Do you like Allan?

LIEUTENANT. The young man is my best pupil, and I value him personally also on account of his strength of character—Yes, life has moments when strength is required [*with emphasis*] to bear up, to endure, to suffer, in a word!

JUDITH. That was more than one word, I should say. However, you like Allan?

LIEUTENANT. Yes.

JUDITH. Look him up then, and keep him company.

LIEUTENANT. It was for that purpose I came here—for that and no other. I had no other object in my visit.

JUDITH. I had not supposed anything of that kind—of the kind you mean!   Allan went that way.

[*Pointing to the left.*

LIEUTENANT. [*Goes reluctantly to the left*] Yes—I'll do what you ask.

JUDITH. Do, please.

ALICE. [*In from the background*] What are you doing here?

JUDITH. I wanted to borrow a wrench.

ALICE. Will you listen to me a moment?

JUDITH. Of course, I will.

[ALICE *sits down on the sofa.*

JUDITH. [*Remains standing*] But tell me quickly what you want to say.   I don't like long lectures.

ALICE. Lectures?   Well, then—put up your hair and put on a long dress.

JUDITH. Why?

ALICE. Because you are no longer a child.   And you are young enough to need no coquetry about your age.

JUDITH. What does that mean?

ALICE. That you have reached marriageable age.   And your way of dressing is causing scandal.

JUDITH. Then I shall do what you say.

ALICE. You have understood then?

JUDITH. Oh, yes.

ALICE. And we are agreed?

JUDITH. Perfectly.

ALICE. On all points?

JUDITH. Even the tenderest!

ALICE. Will you at the same time cease playing—with Allan?

JUDITH. It is going to be serious then?

ALICE. Yes.

JUDITH. Then we may just as well begin at once.

> *She has already laid aside the handle-bars. Now she lets down the bicycle skirt and twists her braid into a knot which she fastens on top of her head with a hair-pin taken out of her mother's hair.*

ALICE. It is not proper to make your toilet in a strange place.

JUDITH. Am I all right this way? Then I am ready. Come now who dares!

ALICE. Now at last you look decent. And leave Allan in peace after this.

JUDITH. I don't understand what you mean?

ALICE. Can't you see that he is suffering?

JUDITH. Yes, I think I have noticed it, but I don't know why. I don't suffer!

ALICE. That is *your* strength. But the day will come—oh, yes, you shall know what it means. Go home now, and don't forget—that you are wearing a long skirt.

JUDITH. Must you walk differently then?

ALICE. Just try.

JUDITH. [*Tries to walk like a lady*] Oh, my feet are tied; I am caught, I cannot run any longer!

ALICE. Yes, child, now the walking begins, along the slow road toward the unknown, which you know already, but must pretend to ignore. Shorter steps, and much slower—much slower! The low shoes of childhood must go, Judith, and you have to wear boots. You don't remember when you laid aside baby socks and put on shoes, but I do!

JUDITH. I can never stand this!

ALICE. And yet you must—must!

JUDITH. [*Goes over to her mother and kisses her lightly on the cheek; then walks out with the dignified bearing of a lady, but forgetting the handle-bars*] Good-bye then!

CURT. [*Enters from the right*] So you're already here?

ALICE. Yes.

CURT. Has *he* come back?

ALICE. Yes.

CURT. How did he appear?

ALICE. In full dress—so he has called on the Colonel. And he wore two orders.

CURT. Two? I knew he was to receive the Order of the Sword on his retirement. But what can the other one be?

ALICE. I am not very familiar with those things, but there was a white cross within a red one.

CURT. It is a Portuguese order then. Let me see—tell me, didn't his articles in that periodical deal with quarantine stations in Portuguese harbours?

ALICE. Yes, as far as I can recall.

CURT. And he has never been in Portugal?

ALICE. Never.

CURT. But I have been there.

ALICE. You shouldn't be so communicative. His ears and his memory are so good.

CURT. Don't you think Judith may have helped him to this honour?

ALICE. Well, I declare! There are limits— [*rising*] and you have passed them.

CURT. Are we to quarrel now?

ALICE. That depends on you. Don't meddle with my interests.

CURT. If they cross my own, I have to meddle with them, although with a careful hand. Here he comes!

ALICE. And now it is going to happen.

CURT. What is—going to happen?

ALICE. We shall see!

CURT. Let it come to open attack then, for this state of siege is getting on my nerves. I have not a friend left on the island.

ALICE. Wait a minute! You sit on this side—he must have the easy-chair, of course—and then I can prompt you.

CAPTAIN. [*Enters from the background, in full dress uniform, wearing the Order of the Sword and the Portuguese Order of Christ*] Good day! Here's the meeting place.

ALICE. You are tired—sit down. [*The* CAPTAIN, *contrary to expectation, takes a seat on the sofa to the left*] Make yourself comfortable.

CAPTAIN. This is all right. You're too kind.

ALICE. [*To* CURT] Be careful—he's suspicious of us.

CAPTAIN. [*Crossly*] What was that you said?

ALICE. [*To* CURT] He must have been drinking.

CAPTAIN. [*Rudely*] No-o, he has not. [*Silence*] Well—how have you been amusing yourselves?

ALICE. And you?

CAPTAIN. Are you looking at my orders?

ALICE. No-o!

CAPTAIN. I guess not, because you are jealous— Otherwise it is customary to offer congratulations to the recipient of honours.

ALICE. We congratulate you.

CAPTAIN. We get things like these instead of laurel wreaths, such as they give to actresses.

ALICE. That's for the wreaths at home on the walls of the tower——

CAPTAIN. Which your brother gave you——

ALICE. Oh, how you talk!

CAPTAIN. Before which I have had to bow down these twenty-five years—and which it has taken me twenty-five years to expose.

ALICE. You have seen my brother?

CAPTAIN. Rather! [ALICE *is crushed. Silence*] And you, Curt—you don't say anything, do you?

CURT. I am waiting.

CAPTAIN. Well, I suppose you know the big news?

CURT. No.

CAPTAIN. It is not exactly agreeable for me to be the one who——

CURT. Oh, speak up!

CAPTAIN. The soda factory has gone to the wall——

CURT. That's decidedly unpleasant! Where does that leave you?

CAPTAIN. I am all right, as I sold out in time.

CURT. That was sensible.

CAPTAIN. But how about you?

CURT. Done for!

CAPTAIN. It's your own fault. You should have sold out in time, or taken new stock.

CURT. So that I could lose that too.

CAPTAIN. No, for then the company would have been all right.

CURT. Not the company, but the directors, for in my mind that new subscription was simply a collection for the benefit of the board.

CAPTAIN. And now I ask whether such a view of the matter will save your money?

CURT. No, I shall have to give up everything.

CAPTAIN. Everything?

CURT. Even my home, the furniture——

CAPTAIN. But that's dreadful!

CURT. I have experienced worse things.   [*Silence.*

CAPTAIN. That's what happens when amateurs want to speculate.

CURT. You surprise me, for you know very well that if I had not subscribed, I should have been boycotted. The supplementary livelihood of the coast population, toilers of the sea, inexhaustible capital, inexhaustible as the sea itself— philanthropy and national prosperity— Thus you wrote and printed— And now you speak of it as speculation!

CAPTAIN. [*Unmoved*] What are you going to do now?

CURT. Have an auction, I suppose.

CAPTAIN. You had better.

CURT. What do you mean?

CAPTAIN. What I said! For there [*slowly*] are going to be some changes——

CURT. On the island?

CAPTAIN. Yes—as, for instance,—your quarters are going to be exchanged for somewhat simpler ones.

CURT. Well, well.

CAPTAIN. Yes, the plan is to place the quarantine station on the outside shore, near the water.

CURT. My original idea!

CAPTAIN. [*Dryly*] I don't know about that—for I am not familiar with your ideas on the subject. However—it seems then quite natural that you dispose of the furniture, and it will attract much less notice—the scandal!

CURT. What?

CAPTAIN. The scandal! [*Egging himself on*] For it is a scandal to come to a new place and immediately get into financial troubles which must result in a lot of annoyance to the relatives—particularly to the relatives.

CURT. Oh, I guess I'll have to bear the worst of it.

CAPTAIN. I'll tell you one thing, my dear Curt: if I had not stood by you in this matter, you would have lost your position.

CURT. That too?

CAPTAIN. It comes rather hard for you to keep things in order—complaints have been made against your work.

CURT. Warranted complaints?

CAPTAIN. Yah! For you are—in spite of your other respectable qualities—a careless fellow— Don't interrupt me!— You are a very careless fellow!

CURT. How strange!

CAPTAIN. However—the suggested change is going to take place very soon.   And I should advise you to hold the auction at once or sell privately.

CURT. Privately?   And where could I find a buyer in this place?

CAPTAIN. Well, I hope you don't expect me to settle down in the midst of your things?   That would make a fine story— [staccato] hm!—especially when I—think of what happened— once upon a time——

CURT. What was that?   Are you referring to what did *not* happen?

CAPTAIN. [*Turning about*] You are so silent, Alice?   What is the matter, old girl?   Not blue, I hope?

ALICE. I sit here and think——

CAPTAIN. Goodness!   Are you thinking?   But you have to think quickly, keenly, and correctly, if it is to be of any help!   So do your thinking now—one, two, three!   Ha-ha! You can't!   Well, then, I must try—   Where is Judith?

ALICE. Somewhere.

CAPTAIN. Where is Allan? [ALICE *remains silent*] Where is the Lieutenant? [ALICE *as before*] I say, Curt—what are you going to do with Allan now?

CURT. Do with him?

CAPTAIN. Yes, you cannot afford to keep him in the artillery now.

CURT. Perhaps not.

CAPTAIN. You had better get him into some cheap infantry regiment—up in Norrland, or somewhere.

CURT. In Norrland?

CAPTAIN. Yes, or suppose you turned him into something practical at once? If I were in your place, I should get him into some business office—why not? [CURT *is silent*] In these enlightened times—yah! Alice is so *uncommonly* silent! Yes, children, this is the seesawing seesaw board of life— one moment high up, looking boldly around, and the next way down, and then upward again, and so on— So much for that— [*To* ALICE] Did you say anything? [ALICE *shakes her head*] We may expect company here in a few days.

ALICE. Were you speaking to me?

CAPTAIN. We may expect company in a few days—notable company!

ALICE. Who?

CAPTAIN. Behold—you're interested! Now you can sit there and guess who is coming, and between guesses you may read this letter over again.   [*Hands her an opened letter.*

ALICE. My letter? Opened? Back from the mail?

CAPTAIN. [*Rising*] Yes, as the head of the family and your guardian, I look after the sacred interests of the family, and with iron hand I shall cut short every effort to break the family ties by means of criminal correspondence. Yah! [ALICE *is crushed*] I am not dead, you know, but don't take offence now because I am going to raise us all out of undeserved humility—undeserved on my own part, at least!

ALICE. Judith! Judith!

CAPTAIN. And Holofernes? I, perhaps? Pooh!

                          [*Goes out through the background.*

CURT. Who is that man?

ALICE. How can I tell?

CURT. We are beaten.

ALICE. Yes—beyond a doubt.

CURT. He has stripped me of everything, but so cleverly that I can accuse him of nothing.

ALICE. Why, no—you owe him a debt of gratitude instead!

CURT. Does he know what he is doing?

ALICE. No, I don't think so. He follows his nature and his instincts, and just now he seems to be in favour where fortune and misfortune are being meted out.

CURT. I suppose it's the Colonel who is to come here.

ALICE. Probably. And that is why Allan must go.

CURT. And you find that right?

ALICE. Yes.

CURT. Then our ways part.

ALICE. [*Ready to go*] A little—but we shall come together again.

CURT. Probably.

ALICE. And do you know where?

CURT. Here.

ALICE. You guess it?

CURT. That's easy! He takes the house and buys the furniture.

ALICE. I think so, too. But don't desert me!

CURT. Not for a little thing like that.

ALICE. Good-bye.   [*Goes.*

CURT. Good-bye.

Curtain.

Same stage setting, but the day is cloudy and it is raining outside. ALICE *and* CURT *enter from the background, wearing rain coats and carrying umbrellas.*

ALICE. At last I have got you to come here! But, I cannot be so cruel as to wish you welcome to your own home——

CURT. Oh, why not? I have passed through three forced sales—and worse than that— It doesn't matter to me.

ALICE. Did he call you?

CURT. It was a formal command, but on what basis I don't understand.

ALICE. Why, he is not your superior!

CURT. No, but he has made himself king of the island. And if there be any resistance, he has only to mention the Colonel's name, and everybody submits. Tell me, is it to-day the Colonel is coming?

ALICE. He is expected—but I know nothing with certainty— Sit down, please.

CURT. [*Sitting down*] Nothing has been changed here.

ALICE. Don't think of it! Don't renew the pain!

CURT. The pain? I find it merely a little strange. Strange as the man himself. Do you know, when I made his acquaintance as a boy, I fled him. But he was after me. Flattered, offered services, and surrounded me with ties— I repeated my attempt at escape, but in vain— And now I am his slave!

ALICE. And why? He owes you a debt, but you appear as the debtor.

CURT. Since I lost all I had, he has offered me help in getting Allan through his examinations——

ALICE. For which you will have to pay dearly! You are still a candidate for the Riksdag?

CURT. Yes, and, so far as I can see, there is nothing in my way.   [Silence.

ALICE. Is Allan really going to leave to-day?

CURT. Yes, if I cannot prevent it.

ALICE. That was a short-lived happiness.

CURT. Short-lived as everything but life itself, which lasts all too long

ALICE. Too long, indeed!— Won't you come in and wait in the sitting-room? Even if it does not trouble you, it troubles me—these surroundings!

CURT. If you wish it——

ALICE. I feel ashamed, so ashamed that I could wish to die —but I can alter nothing!

CURT. Let us go then—as you wish it.

ALICE. And somebody is coming too.

[They go out to the left.

The CAPTAIN and ALLAN enter from the background, both in uniform and wearing cloaks.

CAPTAIN. Sit down, my boy, and let me have a talk with you.   [Sits down in the easy-chair.

[ALLAN sits down on the chair to the left.

CAPTAIN. It's raining to-day—otherwise I could sit here comfortably and look at the sea. [Silence] Well?— You don't like to go, do you?

ALLAN. I don't like to leave my father.

CAPTAIN. Yes, your father—he is rather an unfortunate man. [Silence] And parents rarely understand the true welfare of their children. That is to say—there are exceptions, of course. Hm! Tell me, Allan, have you any communication with your mother?

ALLAN. Yes, she writes now and then

CAPTAIN. Do you know that she is your guardian?

ALLAN. Yes.

CAPTAIN. Now, Allan, do you know that your mother has authorised me to act in her place?

ALLAN. I didn't know that!

CAPTAIN. Well, you know it now. And, therefore, all discussions concerning your career are done with— And you are going to Norrland.

ALLAN. But I have no money.

CAPTAIN. I have arranged for what you need.

ALLAN. All I can do then is to thank you, Uncle.

CAPTAIN. Yes, *you* are grateful—which everybody is not. Hm!— [*Raising his voice*] The Colonel—do you know the Colonel?

ALLAN. [*Embarrassed*] No, I don't.

CAPTAIN. [*With emphasis*] The Colonel—is my special friend—[*a little more hurriedly*] as you know, perhaps. Hm! The Colonel has wished to show his interest in my family, including my wife's relatives. Through his intercession, the Colonel has been able to provide the means needed for the completion of your course. Now you understand the obligation under which you and your father are placed toward the Colonel. Have I spoken with sufficient plainness? [ALLAN *bows*] Go and pack your things now. The money will be handed to you at the landing. And now good-bye, my boy. [*Holds out a finger to* ALLAN] Good-bye then.

> [*Rises and goes out to the right.*

> [ALLAN, *alone, stands still, looking sadly around the room.*

JUDITH. [*Enters from the background, wearing a hooded rain coat and carrying an umbrella; otherwise exquisitely dressed, in long skirt and with her hair put up*] Is that you, Allan!

ALLAN. [*Turning around, surveys* JUDITH *carefully*] Is that you, Judith?

JUDITH. You don't know me any longer? Where have you been all this time? What are you looking at? My long dress—and my hair— You have not seen me like this before?

ALLAN. No-o——

JUDITH. Do I look like a married woman?

[ALLAN *turns away from her.*

JUDITH. [*Earnestly*] What are you doing here?

ALLAN. I am saying good-bye.

JUDITH. What? You are going—away?

ALLAN. I am transferred to Norrland.

JUDITH. [*Dumfounded*] To Norrland? When are you going?

ALLAN. To-day.

JUDITH. Whose doing is this?

ALLAN. Your father's.

JUDITH. That's what I thought! [*Walks up and down the floor, stamping her feet*] I wish you had stayed over to-day.

ALLAN. In order to meet the Colonel?

JUDITH. What do you know about the Colonel?— Is it certain that you are going?

ALLAN. There is no other choice. And now I want it myself. [*Silence.*

JUDITH. Why do you want it now?

ALLAN. I want to get away from here—out into the world!

JUDITH. It's too close here? Yes, Allan, I understand you —it's unbearable here—here, where they speculate—in soda and human beings! [*Silence.*

JUDITH. [*With genuine emotion*] As you know, Allan, I possess that fortunate nature which cannot suffer—but—now I am learning!

ALLAN. You?

JUDITH. Yes—now it's beginning! [*She presses both hands to her breast*] Oh, how it hurts—oh!

ALLAN. What is it?

JUDITH. I don't know—I choke—I think I'm going to die!

ALLAN. Judith?

JUDITH. [*Crying out*] Oh! Is this the way it feels? Is this the way—poor boys!

ALLAN. I should smile, if I were as cruel as you are.

JUDITH. I am not cruel, but I didn't know better— You must not go!

ALLAN. I have to!

JUDITH. Go then—but give me a keepsake!

ALLAN. What have I to give you?

JUDITH. [*With all the seriousness of deepest suffering*] You!— No, I can never live through this! [*Cries out, pressing her breast with both hands*] I suffer, I suffer— What have you done to me? I don't want to live any longer! Allan, don't go—not alone! Let us go together—we'll take the small boat, the little white one—and we'll sail far out, with the main sheet made fast—the wind is high—and we sail till we founder— out there, way out, where there is no eelgrass and no jelly-fish— What do you say?— But we should have washed the sails yesterday—they should be white as snow—for I want to see white in that moment—and you swim with your arm about me until you grow tired—and then we sink— [*Turning around*] There would be style in that, a good deal more style than in going about here lamenting and smuggling letters that will be opened and jeered at by father— Allan! [*She takes hold of both his arms and shakes him*] Do you hear?

ALLAN. [*Who has been watching her with shining eyes*] Judith! Judith! Why were you not like this before?

JUDITH. I didn't know—how could I tell what I didn't know?

ALLAN. And now I must go away from you! But I sup-

pose it is the better, the only thing! I cannot compete with
a man—like——

JUDITH. Don't speak of the Colonel!

ALLAN. Is it not true?

JUDITH. It is true—and it is not true.

ALLAN. Can it become wholly untrue?

JUDITH. Yes, so it shall—within an hour!

ALLAN. And you keep your word? I can wait, I can suffer,
I can work—Judith!

JUDITH. Don't go yet! How long must I wait?

ALLAN. A year.

JUDITH. [*Exultantly*] One? I shall wait a thousand years,
and if you do not come then, I shall turn the dome of heaven
upside down and make the sun rise in the west— Hush,
somebody is coming! Allan, we must part—take me into
your arms! [*They embrace each other*] But you must not kiss
me. [*Turns her head away*] There, go now! Go now!

> ALLAN *goes toward the background and puts on his cloak.
> Then they rush into each other's arms so that* JUDITH
> *disappears beneath the cloak, and for a moment they
> exchange kisses.* ALLAN *rushes out.* JUDITH *throws
> herself face downward on the sofa and sobs.*

ALLAN. [*Comes back and kneels beside the sofa*] No, I cannot go! I cannot go away from you—not now!

JUDITH. [*Rising*] If you could only see how beautiful you
are now! If you could only see yourself!

ALLAN. Oh, no, a man cannot be beautiful. But you, Judith! You—that you—oh, I saw that, when you were kind,
another Judith appeared—and she's mine!— But if you
don't keep faith with me now, then I shall die!

JUDITH. I think I am dying even now— Oh, that I
might die now, just now, when I am so happy——

ALLAN. Somebody is coming!

JUDITH. Let them come!   I fear nothing in the world here-after.   But I wish you could take me along under your cloak. [*She hides herself in play under his cloak*] And then I should fly with you to Norrland.   What are we to do in Norrland? Become a Fusilier—one of those that wear plumes on their hats?   There's style in that, and it will be becoming to you.

[*Plays with his hair.*

ALLAN *kisses the tips of her fingers, one by one—and then he kisses her shoe.*

JUDITH. What are you doing, Mr. Madcap?   Your lips will get black. [*Rising impetuously*] And then I cannot kiss you when you go!   Come, and I'll go with you!

ALLAN. No, then I should be placed under arrest.

JUDITH. I'll go with you to the guard-room.

ALLAN. They wouldn't let you!   We must part now!

JUDITH. I am going to swim after the steamer—and then you jump in and save me—and it gets into the newspapers, and we become engaged.   Shall we do that?

ALLAN. You can still jest?

JUDITH. There will always be time for tears—   Say good-bye now!——

They rush into each other's arms; then ALLAN with-draws slowly through the door in the background, JUDITH following him; the door remains open after them; they embrace again outside, in the rain.

ALLAN. You'll get wet, Judith.

JUDITH. What do I care!

They tear themselves away from each other.   ALLAN leaves.   JUDITH remains behind, exposing herself to the rain and to the wind, which strains at her hair and her clothes while she is waving her handkerchief. Then JUDITH runs back into the room and throws herself on the sofa, with her face buried in her hands.

ALICE. [*Enters and goes over to* JUDITH] What is this?—
Get up and let me look at you.

[JUDITH *sits up.*

ALICE. [*Scrutinising her*] You are not sick— And I am
not going to console you.   [*Goes out to the right.*

The LIEUTENANT *enters from the background.*

JUDITH. [*Gets up and puts on the hooded coat*] Come along
to the telegraph office, Lieutenant.

LIEUTENANT. If I can be of any service—but I don't think
it's quite proper——

JUDITH. So much the better! I want you to compromise
me—but without any illusions on your part— Go ahead,
please!   [*They go out through the background.*

The CAPTAIN and ALICE *enter from the right; he is in
undress uniform.*

CAPTAIN. [*Sits down in the easy-chair*] Let him come in.

ALICE *goes over to the door on the left and opens it,
whereupon she sits down on the sofa.*

CURT. [*Enters from the left*] You want to speak to me?

CAPTAIN. [*Pleasantly, but somewhat condescendingly*] Yes,
I have quite a number of important things to tell you. Sit
down.

CURT. [*Sits down on the chair to the left*] I am all ears.

CAPTAIN. Well, then!— [*Bumptiously*] You know that our
quarantine system has been neglected during nearly a century—hm!

ALICE. [*To* CURT] That's the candidate for the Riksdag
who speaks now.

CAPTAIN. But with the tremendous development witnessed
by our own day in——

ALICE. [*To* CURT] The communications, of course!

CAPTAIN. —all kinds of ways the government has begun

to consider improvements. And for this purpose the Board of Health has appointed inspectors—hm!

ALICE. [*To* CURT] He's giving dictation.

CAPTAIN. You may as well learn it now as later—I have been appointed an inspector of quarantines.   [*Silence.*

CURT. I congratulate—and pay my respects to my superior at the same time.

CAPTAIN. On account of ties of kinship our personal relations will remain unchanged. However—to speak of other things— At my request your son Allan has been transferred to an infantry regiment in Norrland.

CURT. But I don't want it.

CAPTAIN. Your will in this case is subordinate to the mother's wishes—and as the mother has authorised me to decide, I have formed this decision.

CURT. I admire you!

CAPTAIN. Is that the only feeling you experience at this moment when you are to part from your son? Have you no other purely human feelings?

CURT. You mean that I ought to be suffering?

CAPTAIN. Yes.

CURT. It would please you if I suffered. You wish me to suffer.

CAPTAIN. *You* suffer?— Once I was taken sick—you were present and I can still remember that your face expressed nothing but undisguised pleasure.

ALICE. That is not true! Curt sat beside your bed all night and calmed you down when your qualms of conscience became too violent—but when you recovered you ceased to be thankful for it——

CAPTAIN. [*Pretending not to hear* ALICE] Consequently Allan will have to leave us.

CURT. And who is going to pay for it?

CAPTAIN. I have done so already—that is to say, we—a syndicate of people interested in the young man's future.

CURT. A syndicate?

CAPTAIN. Yes—and to make sure that everything is all right you can look over these subscription lists.

[*Hands him some papers.*

CURT. Lists? [*Reading the papers*] These are begging letters?

CAPTAIN. Call them what you please.

CURT. Have you gone begging on behalf of my son?

CAPTAIN. Are you ungrateful again?   An ungrateful man is the heaviest burden borne by the earth.

CURT. Then I am dead socially! And my candidacy is done for!

CAPTAIN. What candidacy?

CURT. For the Riksdag, of course.

CAPTAIN. I hope you never had any such notions—particularly as you might have guessed that I, as an older resident, intended to offer my own services, which you seem to underestimate.

CURT. Oh, well, then that's gone, too!

CAPTAIN. It doesn't seem to trouble you very much.

CURT. Now you have taken everything—do you want more?

CAPTAIN. Have you anything more? And have you anything to reproach me with? Consider carefully if you have anything to reproach me with.

CURT. Strictly speaking, no! Everything has been correct and legal as it should be between honest citizens in the course of daily life——

CAPTAIN. You say this with a resignation which I would call cynical. But your entire nature has a cynical bent, my dear Curt, and there are moments when I feel tempted to share Alice's opinion of you—that you are a hypocrite, a hypo-crite of the first water.

CURT. [*Calmly*] So that's Alice's opinion?

ALICE. [*To* CURT] It was—once. But not now, for it takes true heroism to bear what you have borne—or it takes some-thing else!

CAPTAIN. Now I think the discussion may be regarded as closed. You, Curt, had better go and say good-bye to Allan, who is leaving with the next boat.

CURT. [*Rising*] So soon? Well, I have gone through worse things than that.

CAPTAIN. You say that so often that I am beginning to wonder what you went through in America?

CURT. What I went through? I went through misfortunes. And it is the unmistakable right of every human being to suffer misfortune.

CAPTAIN. [*Sharply*] There are self-inflicted misfortunes— were yours of that kind?

CURT. Is not this a question of conscience?

CAPTAIN. [*Brusquely*] Do you mean to say you have a con-science?

CURT. There are wolves and there are sheep, and no human being is honoured by being a sheep. But I'd rather be that than a wolf!

CAPTAIN. You don't recognise the old truth, that every-body is the maker of his own fortune?

CURT. Is *that* a truth?

CAPTAIN. And you don't know that a man's own strength——

CURT. Yes, I know that from the night when your own strength failed you, and you lay flat on the floor.

CAPTAIN. [*Raising his voice*] A deserving man like myself —yes, look at me— For fifty years I have fought—against a world—but at last I have won the game, by perseverance, loyalty, energy, and—integrity!

ALICE. You should leave that to be said by others!

CAPTAIN. The others won't say it because they are jealous. However—we are expecting company—my daughter Judith will to-day meet her intended— Where is Judith?

ALICE. She is out.

CAPTAIN. In the rain? Send for her.

CURT. Perhaps I may go now?

CAPTAIN. No, you had better stay. Is Judith dressed—Properly?

ALICE. Oh, so-so— Have you definite word from the Colonel that he is coming?

CAPTAIN. [*Rising*] Yes—that is to say, he will take us by surprise, as it is termed. And I am expecting a telegram from him—any moment. [*Goes to the right*] I'll be back at once.

ALICE. There you see him as he is! Can he be called human?

CURT. When you asked that question once before, I answered no. Now I believe him to be the commonest kind of human being of the sort that possess the earth. Perhaps we, too, are of the same kind—making use of other people and of favourable opportunities?

ALICE. He has eaten you and yours alive—and you defend him?

CURT. I have suffered worse things. And this man-eater has left my soul unharmed—*that* he couldn't swallow!

ALICE. What "worse" have you suffered?

CURT. And *you* ask that?

ALICE. Do you wish to be rude?

CURT. No, I don't wish to—and therefore—don't ask again!

CAPTAIN. [*Enters from the right*] The telegram was already there, however— Please read it, Alice, for I cannot see— [*Seats himself pompously in the easy-chair*] Read it! You need not go, Curt.

> ALICE *glances through the telegram quickly and looks perplexed.*

CAPTAIN. Well? Don't you find it pleasing?

> [ALICE *stares in silence at the* CAPTAIN.

CAPTAIN. [*Ironically*] Who is it from?

ALICE. From the Colonel.

CAPTAIN. [*With self-satisfaction*] So I thought—and what does the Colonel say?

ALICE. This is what he says: "On account of Miss Judith's impertinent communication over the telephone, I consider the relationship ended—for ever!"

> [*Looks intently at the* CAPTAIN.

CAPTAIN. Once more, if you please.

ALICE. [*Reads rapidly*] "On account of Miss Judith's impertinent communication over the telephone, I consider the relationship ended—for ever!"

CAPTAIN. [*Turns pale*] It is Judith!

ALICE. And there is Holofernes!

CAPTAIN. And what are you?

ALICE. Soon you will see!

CAPTAIN. This is your doing!

ALICE. No!

CAPTAIN. [*In a rage*] This is your doing!

ALICE. No! [*The* CAPTAIN *tries to rise and draw his sabre, but falls back, touched by an apoplectic stroke*] There you got what was coming to you!

CAPTAIN. [*With senile tears in his voice*] Don't be angry at me— I am very sick——

ALICE. Are you? I am glad to hear it.

CURT. Let us put him to bed.

ALICE. No, I don't want to touch him.   [*Rings*

CAPTAIN. [*As before*] You must not be angry at me! [*To
CURT*] Look after my children!

CURT. This is sublime! I am to look after his children,
and he has stolen mine!

ALICE. Always the same self-deception!

CAPTAIN. Look after my children! [*Continues to mumble
unintelligibly*] Blub-blub-blub-blub.

ALICE. At last that tongue is checked! Can brag no more,
lie no more, wound no more! You, Curt, who believe in God,
give Him thanks on my behalf. Thank Him for my liberation
from the tower, from the wolf, from the vampire!

CURT. Not that way, Alice!

ALICE. [*With her face close to the* CAPTAIN's] Where is your
own strength now? Tell me? Where is your energy? [*The
CAPTAIN, speechless, spits in her face*] Oh, you can still squirt
venom, you viper—then I'll tear the tongue out of your throat!
[*Cuffs him on the ear*] The head is off, but still it blushes!—
O, Judith, glorious girl, whom I have carried like vengeance
under my heart—you, you have set us free, all of us!— If
you have more heads than one, Hydra, we'll take them! [*Pulls
his beard*] Think only that justice exists on the earth! Sometimes I dreamed it, but I could never believe it. Curt, ask
God to pardon me for misjudging Him. Oh, there is justice!
So I will become a sheep, too! Tell Him that, Curt! A
little success makes us better, but adversity alone turns us
into wolves.

The LIEUTENANT *enters from the background.*

ALICE. The Captain has had a stroke—will you please help
us to roll out the chair?

LIEUTENANT. Madam——

ALICE. What is it?

LIEUTENANT. Well, Miss Judith——

ALICE. Help us with this first—then you can speak of Miss Judith afterward.

[*The* LIEUTENANT *rolls out the chair to the right.*

ALICE. Away with the carcass! Out with it, and let's open the doors! The place must be aired! [*Opens the doors in the background; the sky has cleared*] Ugh!

CURT. Are you going to desert him?

ALICE. A wrecked ship is deserted, and the crew save their lives—I'll not act as undertaker to a rotting beast! Drainmen and dissectors may dispose of him! A garden bed would be too good for that barrowful of filth! Now I am going to wash and bathe myself in order to get rid of all this impurity—if I can ever cleanse myself completely!

JUDITH *is seen outside, by the balustrade, waving her handkerchief toward the sea.*

CURT. [*Toward the background*] Who is there? Judith! [*Calls out*] Judith!

JUDITH. [*Cries out as she enters*] He is gone!

CURT. Who?

JUDITH. Allan is gone!

CURT. Without saying good-bye?

JUDITH. He did to me, and he sent his love to you, Uncle.

ALICE. Oh, that was it!

JUDITH. [*Throwing herself into* CURT's *arms*] He is gone!

CURT. He will come back, little girl.

ALICE. Or we will go after him!

CURT. [*With a gesture indicating the door on the right*] And leave him? What would the world——

ALICE. The world—bah! Judith, come into my arms! [JUDITH *goes up to* ALICE, *who kisses her on the forehead*] Do you want to go after him?

JUDITH. How can you ask?

ALICE. But your father is sick.

JUDITH. What do I care!

ALICE. This is Judith! Oh, I love you, Judith!

JUDITH. And besides, papa is never mean—and he doesn't like cuddling. There's style to papa, after all.

ALICE. Yes, in a way!

JUDITH. And I don't think he is longing for me after that telephone message— Well, why should he pester me with an old fellow? No, Allan, Allan! [*Throws herself into* CURT's *arms*] I want to go to Allan!

> *Tears herself loose again and runs out to wave her hand-*
> *kerchief.*

> [CURT *follows her and waves his handkerchief also.*

ALICE. Think of it, that flowers can grow out of dirt!

> *The* LIEUTENANT *in from the right.*

ALICE. Well?

LIEUTENANT. Yes, Miss Judith——

ALICE. Is the feeling of those letters that form her name so sweet on your lips that it makes you forget him who is dying?

LIEUTENANT. Yes, but she said——

ALICE. She? Say rather Judith then! But first of all—how goes it in there?

LIEUTENANT. Oh, in there—it's all over!

ALICE. All over? O, God, on my own behalf and that of all mankind, I thank Thee for having freed us from this evil! Your arm, if you please—I want to go outside and get a breath—breathe!

> [*The* LIEUTENANT *offers his arm.*

ALICE. [*Checks herself*] Did he say anything before the end came?

LIEUTENANT. Miss Judith's father spoke a few words only.

ALICE. What did he say?

LIEUTENANT. He said: "Forgive them, for they know not what they do!"

ALICE. Inconceivable!

LIEUTENANT. Yes, Miss Judith's father was a good and noble man.

ALICE. Curt!

CURT *Enters.*

ALICE. It is over!

CURT. Oh!

ALICE. Do you know what his last words were? No, you can never guess it. "Forgive them, for they know not what they do!"

CURT. Can you translate it?

ALICE. I suppose he meant that he had always done right and died as one that had been wronged by life.

CURT. I am sure his funeral sermon will be fine.

ALICE. And plenty of flowers—from the non-commissioned officers.

CURT. Yes.

ALICE. About a year ago he said something like this: "It looks to me as if life were a tremendous hoax played on all of us!"

CURT. Do you mean to imply that he was playing a hoax on us up to the very moment of death?

ALICE. No—but now, when he is dead, I feel a strange inclination to speak well of him.

CURT. Well, let us do so!

LIEUTENANT. Miss Judith's father was a good and noble man.

ALICE. [*To* CURT] Listen to that!

CURT. "They know not what they do." How many times did I not ask you whether he knew what he was doing? And you didn't think he knew. Therefore, forgive him!

ALICE. Riddles! Riddles! But do you notice that there is peace in the house now? The wonderful peace of death. Wonderful as the solemn anxiety that surrounds the coming of a child into the world. I hear the silence—and on the floor I see the traces of the easy-chair that carried him away— And I feel that now my own life is ended, and I am starting on the road to dissolution! Do you know, it's queer, but those simple words of the Lieutenant—and his is a simple mind—they pursue me, but now they have become serious. My husband, my youth's beloved—yes, perhaps you laugh!—he *was* a good and noble man—nevertheless!

CURT. Nevertheless? And a brave one—as he fought for his own and his family's existence!

ALICE. What worries! What humiliations! Which he wiped out—in order to pass on!

CURT. He was one who had been passed by! And that is to say much! Alice, go in there!

ALICE. No, I cannot do it! For while we have been talking here, the image of him as he was in his younger years has come back to me—I have seen him, I see him—now, as when he was only twenty—I must have loved that man!

CURT. And hated him!

ALICE. And hated!— Peace be with him!

> Goes toward the right door and stops in front of it, folding her hands as if to pray.

Curtain.